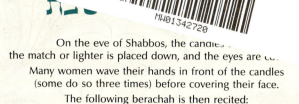

On the eve of Shabbos, the candles are lit, the match or lighter is placed down, and the eyes are covered. Many women wave their hands in front of the candles (some do so three times) before covering their face.

The following berachah is then recited:

בָּרוּךְ אַתָּה יהוה אֱלֹהֵינוּ מֶלֶךְ הָעוֹלָם אֲשֶׁר קִדְּשָׁנוּ בְּמִצְוֹתָיו וְצִוָּנוּ לְהַדְלִיק נֵר שֶׁל שַׁבָּת.

It is customary to recite the following prayer after the kindling. The words in brackets are included as they apply.

יְהִי רָצוֹן לְפָנֶיךָ, יהוה אֱלֹהַי וֵאלֹהֵי אֲבוֹתַי, שֶׁתְּחוֹנֵן אוֹתִי [וְאֶת אִישִׁי, וְאֶת בָּנַי, וְאֶת בְּנוֹתַי, וְאֶת אָבִי, וְאֶת אִמִּי] וְאֶת כָּל קְרוֹבַי; וְתִתֶּן לָנוּ וּלְכָל יִשְׂרָאֵל חַיִּים טוֹבִים וַאֲרוּכִים; וְתִזְכְּרֵנוּ בְּזִכְרוֹן טוֹבָה וּבְרָכָה; וְתִפְקְדֵנוּ בִּפְקֻדַּת יְשׁוּעָה וְרַחֲמִים; וּתְבָרְכֵנוּ בְּרָכוֹת גְּדוֹלוֹת; וְתַשְׁלִים בָּתֵּינוּ; וְתַשְׁכֵּן שְׁכִינָתְךָ בֵּינֵינוּ. וְזַכֵּנִי לְגַדֵּל בָּנִים וּבְנֵי בָנִים חֲכָמִים וּנְבוֹנִים, אוֹהֲבֵי ה', יִרְאֵי אֱלֹהִים, אַנְשֵׁי אֱמֶת, זֶרַע קֹדֶשׁ, בַּה' דְּבֵקִים, וּמְאִירִים אֶת הָעוֹלָם בַּתּוֹרָה וּבְמַעֲשִׂים טוֹבִים, וּבְכָל מְלֶאכֶת עֲבוֹדַת הַבּוֹרֵא. אָנָּא שְׁמַע אֶת תְּחִנָּתִי בָּעֵת הַזֹּאת, בִּזְכוּת שָׂרָה וְרִבְקָה וְרָחֵל וְלֵאָה אִמּוֹתֵינוּ, וְהָאֵר נֵרֵנוּ שֶׁלֹּא יִכְבֶּה לְעוֹלָם וָעֶד, וְהָאֵר פָּנֶיךָ וְנִוָּשֵׁעָה. אָמֵן.

Candle Lighting for Yom Tov appears inside the back cover.

ArtScroll® Series

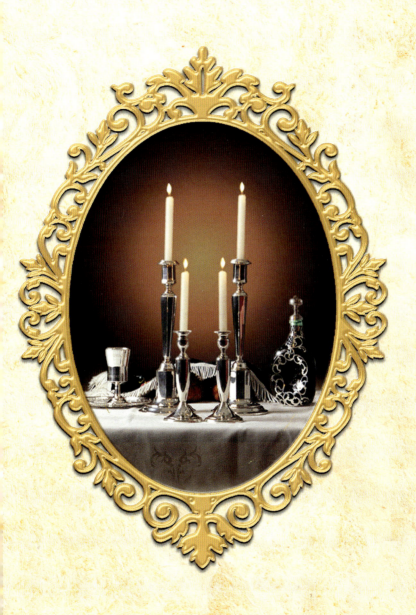

Rabbi Nosson Scherman / Rabbi Gedaliah Zlotowitz
General Editors
Rabbi Meir Zlotowitz ז"ל, Founder and President

THE EISHES CHAYIL CANDLE

Published by
ArtScroll®
Mesorah Publications, ltd

הדלקת הנרות

Lighting Treasury

by Rabbi Dov Weller

Foreword by
Rabbi Warren Goldstein

ARTSCROLL® SERIES

"THE EISHES CHAYIL CANDLE LIGHTING TREASURY"

© Copyright 2017 by Mesorah Publications, Ltd.

First edition — First impression: August, 2017

ALL RIGHTS RESERVED

No part of this book may be reproduced **in any form,** photocopy, electronic media, or otherwise — even FOR PERSONAL, STUDY GROUP, OR CLASSROOM USE — without **written** permission from the copyright holder, except by a reviewer who wishes to quote brief passages in connection with a review written for inclusion in magazines or newspapers.

THE RIGHTS OF THE COPYRIGHT HOLDER WILL BE STRICTLY ENFORCED.

Published by **MESORAH PUBLICATIONS, LTD.**
4401 Second Avenue / Brooklyn, NY 11232 / (718) 921-9000
www.artscroll.com / comments@artscroll.com

Distributed in Israel by SIFRIATI / A. GITLER
POB 2351 / Bnei Brak 51122

Distributed in Europe by LEHMANNS
Unit E, Viking Business Park, Rolling Mill Road /
Jarrow, Tyne and Wear NE32 3DP / England

Distributed in Australia and New Zealand by
GOLDS WORLD OF JUDAICA
3-13 William Street / Balaclava, Melbourne 3183 / Victoria Australia

Distributed in South Africa by KOLLEL BOOKSHOP
Northfield Centre, 17 Northfield Avenue / Glenhazel 2192 /
Johannesburg, South Africa

ISBN 10: 1-4226-1921-4 / ISBN 13: 978-1-4226-1921-6
(Hard Cover)

ISBN 10: 1-4226-1922-2 / ISBN 13: 978-1-4226-1922-3
(Deluxe Hand-tooled Leather)

This volume is dedicated
in memory of
שיינדל מלכה
בת ר' אברהם ראובן ע"ה
כ"ג ניסן תשע"ו

As a young woman in the 1920's she was surrounded by a society and a culture completely antithetical to Yiddishkeit — yet she never wavered.

With no other options, she attended public school and eventually joined the workforce — but her *Yiddishe shtoltz* and fierce commitment to Torah observance were unyielding.

While others forsook the beauty and sanctity of Shabbos, she faithfully kindled the Shabbos candles, opening her heart to welcome the Shabbos Queen into her home. Her well-worn, tear-saturated Sefer Tehillim bears silent but eloquent testimony to her passionate devotion to Hashem. Indeed, she merited raising a beautiful Torah-true family with descendants who are exemplary bnei Torah.

It was the heroism and dedication of such unsung heroes that laid the foundation of Shabbos observance for subsequent generations.

May her memory be a blessing for all of us.

תנצב"ה

Contents

Introduction — 8

Acknowledgments — 9

Foreword — 12

The Light of Shabbos — 15

Shabbos — An Island of Peace / Shabbos Candles and the Jewish Woman / The Inextinguishable Light / Remaining on the Island — Despite the Challenge

Erev Shabbos Kodesh — 23

To Welcome the Shabbos Come, Let Us Go / Shabbos — The Healing Balm and Elixir of Life / Please Protect the Shabbos / Accepting the Shabbos with Love / Better One Less Cake for Shabbos / Giving Up Is Winning / Charity Before Candle Lighting / Accepting Shabbos with a *Chessed*

Candle Lighting — 35

The Berachah, Impact, and Merits of Hadlakas Neiros Shabbos / Origins and Reasons for the Mitzvah of Lighting Candles on Erev Shabbos / Selected Laws and Customs of Shabbos Candle Lighting / How Many Candles Should a Woman Light and Why? / Candlesticks and Candles / Why Was the Mitzvah of Lighting Shabbos Candles Given Specifically to Women? / Hadlakas Neiros

Illuminate the World — 47

The Eternity of the Shabbos Candles / The Shabbos Candles that Burned All Week / From Darkness to Light / Shabbos Candles and Shalom Bayis / Me, You, and Us — The Lesson of the Candles / The Penetrating Message of the Shabbos Candles / Seeing Is Tasting / The Light of Creation, the Light of the Shabbos Candles / Every Child Brings into the Home and the World a Special Light / Light Amidst the Dark / To Search with a Candle / The Candle of Hashem Is the Soul of Man / The Power of Candle Lighting / The Role of a Wife and Mother: Igniting the Spiritual Flames of Her Family / Here Lives a Jew! / Candle Lighting — A Special Time for Prayer / Davening for Anything / A Time to Daven or … / Davening for Others / Thank You, Hashem, for a Beautiful Week / The Power of Tefillos to Kindle the Soul / A Warm Tear / The Everlasting Light of the Shabbos Candles / The Memory of a Mother's Shabbos Candle Tefillos / The Power of a Mother's Tefillos at Candle Lighting / Lighting Up the World / The Tears of a Mother Melt the Hardest of Hearts / The Birth of Shmuel Hanavi and Tefillas Chanah

Yom Tov Candle Lighting — 91

When to Light / When to Recite the Berachah / The Blessings on the Yom Tov Candles / Shehecheyanu

Introduction

When seeking to conjure up in one's mind the vivid imagery of the grandeur of Shabbos and the Jewish woman, one icon inevitably emerges at the forefront. This image is a woman standing over her Shabbos candles, her hands covering her eyes, deep in concentration as she pours her heart out in prayer at this special time. It is for good reason that the Shabbos candles are the symbol that invokes this connection to Shabbos and the Jewish woman, both fundamental components of Jewish existence. The mitzvah of lighting Shabbos candles is widely and proudly practiced across the spectrum of Jewish observance and has been faithfully perpetuated throughout the duration of our long history. This mitzvah ushers in the Shabbos, welcoming the majestic Shabbos Queen with its warm and serene glow. It bestows the serenity and calm within the home that are so integral in creating the atmosphere befitting to greet her. The light of these candles has withstood the test of time and the winds that have sought to blow out its inextinguishable flame.

I consider it a merit to present to the ArtScroll readership a book dedicated to explaining the meaning, importance, and inspiration of *Hadlakas Neiros Shabbos,* as well as to relate the exceptional power and auspiciousness for prayer at this time. I am overcome with deep gratitude to Hashem for having granted me the opportunity to author a work devoted to explaining one of the cornerstone mitzvos of the Jewish nation. This is a task that I have approached with anticipation and emotion.

Throughout writing this work, I attempted to remain true to my goal of providing inspiring stories, practical guidance, and understandable concepts regarding this extraordinary and precious mitzvah. This book is small in size and can be conveniently kept near one's Shabbos candles. Since each segment encapsulates a specific message, much inspiration can be gleaned with investing just a few minutes of reading time. Each self-contained section can be enjoyed independently as time permits, or as a quick source of inspiration at the momentous time of candle lighting. In addition, there is a section detailing selected laws and customs that is intended to serve as an overview and instructional guide to the mitzvah's performance. It is important to keep in mind that the summary of laws is not intended to be comprehensive, and one should ask his/her Rabbi regarding specific scenarios and details that are beyond the scope of this work.

It is my *tefillah* to Hashem that this book serve as a vehicle to inspire its readers to perform this special mitzvah with a more profound understanding of its importance, meaning, and essence. May the greater awareness of the centrality of prayer at the time of *Hadlakas Neiros* serve as a catalyst for our *tefillos* to be answered and a conduit for us and our families to draw closer to our Creator.

Acknowledgments

The light of a candle is only brought to fruition through its various parts — oil, wick, and flame — joining together. The same can be said of this work. It was the invaluable input, insight, and encouragement of many people that resulted in this *sefer* becoming a reality.

My deepest thanks to **Rabbi Avrohom Biderman** of ArtScroll for his personal involvement in all aspects of this project. Thank you to **Rabbi Nosson Scherman,** who took the time to review the manuscript and provide valuable encouragement and feedback. **Chief Rabbi Warren Goldstein** graciously gave of his immensely scarce time to pen a beautiful foreword that has greatly enhanced this *sefer*. Among his visionary and innovative endeavors that have touched the lives of so many, Rabbi Goldstein founded and spearheads the Shabbos Project, a Shabbos awareness program that spans the globe, positively impacting thousands of Jews. May the merit of Shabbos continue to bless him, his family, and his congregation with success and *berachah*.

The appearance of this book is a credit to the talent of **Eli Kroen**, who is responsible for the beautiful page and cover design.

Thank you to **Rabbi Moshe Bamberger**, an inspiring author, for your ideas, pointing me to sources, and involvement in this project. Much appreciation to **Rabbi Avrohom Braun** for reviewing the manuscript and for always being there to provide timely advice and to exchange *divrei Torah*. Thank you to **Rabbi Mordechai Frankel**, **Rabbi Shimon Finkelman**, **Rabbi Dovid Yisroel Weinbaum,** and **Rabbi Kalman Redisch** for taking time to provide insight and assistance that helped shape this *sefer*. I am grateful to **R' Yosef Avrohom Hurwitz**, a valued friend, for your literary support and insight. My *chavrusa*, **Rabbi Moshe Sherrow**, author of the ArtScroll "What If" series, provided insightful suggestions and comments and is owed a debt of appreciation for being one of the first people to encourage me to publish my ideas.

Sincere thanks to **Rebbetzin Debbie Greenblatt** for reviewing the manuscript and providing constructive advice and critique that enhanced this work. I would like to thank **Rebbetzin Sarah Meisels** for her insightful suggestions, encouragement, and overall assistance. Much appreciation to **Mrs. Lori Palatnick**, a visionary leader in Jewish women's education, who took time from her demanding schedule to provide meaningful guidance and input.

Heartfelt thanks to my dear parents, **Dr. Judah and Harriet Weller,** who embody the positive attributes of a candle by constantly providing us with light and warmth. Your love, encouragement, and support serve to illuminate for us a life path that is full of meaning and constant striving to achieve. Thank you, Mommy, for reviewing the manuscript and for providing insightful feedback.

To my in-laws, **Dr. Eli and Feige Mayer**, thank you for your constant support, encouragement, and continuous vote of confidence. Ima, thank you for spending a long flight to Eretz Yisrael reviewing the manuscript.

After publishing the *Eishes Chayil Haggadah* this

past year and experiencing firsthand the myriad steps, details, stresses, and worries that go into authoring a book, the thought of starting the process anew was not at the forefront of my mind. The one to thank for infusing me with the spirit and encouragement necessary to begin this project was my wife, **Rochel**. Thank you for your ever-present inspiration, devotion, and support and for reviewing the manuscript more times than I can count. It is your special attention to the mitzvah of Shabbos candles and your *tefillos* at this time that are the inspiration of this work. May Hashem grant us, our family, and all of *Klal Yisrael* the merit to bask in the radiance of the Shabbos candles and may we experience the fulfillment of the *tefillah* recited at candle lighting: וְזַכֵּנִי לְגַדֵּל בָּנִים וּבְנֵי בָנִים חֲכָמִים וּנְבוֹנִים, אוֹהֲבֵי ה', יְרְאֵי אֱלֹקִים, אַנְשֵׁי אֱמֶת, זֶרַע קֹדֶשׁ, בַּה' דְּבֵקִים, וּמְאִירִים אֶת הָעוֹלָם בַּתּוֹרָה וּבְמַעֲשִׂים טוֹבִים, וּבְכָל מְלֶאכֶת עֲבוֹדַת הַבּוֹרֵא — *Privilege me to raise children and grandchildren who are wise and understanding, who love Hashem and fear God, people of truth, holy offspring, attached to Hashem, who illuminate the world with Torah and good deeds and with every labor in the service of the Creator.*

The author dedicates this work to:

אברהם יצחק בן יחזקאל הכהן ע"ה

כ"ט ניסן תשל"ג

ואשתו

חנה מלכה בת משה ע"ה

ג' חשון תש"מ

דוב בן אברהם יואל ע"ה

י"ד אייר תשמ"ה

יוסף צבי בן שמעון ע"ה

י"ג אדר תשע"ג

מנחם מענדל בן אלתר שמואל אהרן ע"ה

י' חשון תשע"ז

Foreword

To live in darkness is an affliction, one of the worst afflictions. As the plagues struck Egypt with increasing ferocity, the penultimate one was the plague of darkness. Its level of suffering was second only to that inflicted by the tenth plague. Dispelling darkness is a sacred mission and goes to the heart of creation. The earth was a place of "chaos and void and darkness over the abyss" when Hashem made a dramatic transformation by saying, "Let there be light."

The Chafetz Chaim writes that we can learn from Hashem about how light dispels darkness. In the same way that God brought light into a dark world, so too are we called upon to bring light into the world. The Chafetz Chaim points out that the creation of light was at the very beginning of creation because without it nothing else can exist. And so too when it comes to the light of Torah. The Gemara (*Sotah* 21a) compares this world to a dark forest filled with confusion, obstacles, and dangers. The light of the Torah dispels the darkness, as the verse says, "For the mitzvah is a flame and the Torah is light" (*Mishlei* 6:23). Every mitzvah we do sheds some light in our lives. The Gemara states that learning Torah is particularly powerful — when we learn Torah it is like the sun rising over the dark forest illuminating signposts that guide our path. With every act of good we do in the world, we bring more and more light into the world, and we fulfill our mission of dispelling the darkness.

Shabbos has a special power to bring light into the world. And this is the message of our Shabbos candles: that through mitzvos and through holiness, in general, and through Shabbos in particular, we bring light to all of Creation. There are two elements especially to which the Shabbos candles forcefully give expression. There is the fact that candle lighting is a mitzvah that is done in our homes. This means that the place where our duty to spread light begins is our home, and the light we kindle will shine from our home out to the rest of the world. Nurturing holy families, raising children with Torah values, are crucial to what it means to be a Jew. The light of the Shabbos candles represents bringing the light of kindness, connection to Hashem, and the light of mitzvos into the world.

In addition, the light is brought into the home specifically through the power of women who have a unique ability to draw light into this world. At the most critical junctures of history it has been the women that have saved *Klal Yisrael*. Our Sages teach that it was in the merit of the righteous women of that generation that we were redeemed from Egypt. It was the women who did not participate in the sins of the golden calf and the spies. The mitzvah of Shabbos candles propels women into the forefront of making the world into a better place for all.

The world in which we live needs the light of Shabbos more than ever before. It is a world of dislocation and fragmentation and pressure. And into this world Shabbos brings a message of cohesiveness, of togetherness, and of unity. The holiness of Shabbos brings husband and wife together, and brings parents and children together in a spirit of unity. It brings communities together and holds all of us in its loving embrace. The light of Shabbos connects us to Hashem and reminds us that He is our Creator and that He loves us and cares for us. The light of Shabbos helps us to reconnect with ourselves. In the pressure of daily life we actually become disconnected from our own essence and on Shabbos we reconnect with our very own *neshamah*. The light of Shabbos replaces a world of darkness and fragmentation with a world of light and togetherness.

This is a book dedicated to spreading light. It reflects the power of the Shabbos candles and all that they represent to dispel all forms of darkness. I would like to thank Rabbi Dov Weller for honoring

me with the invitation to write a few words of introduction to his thoughtful and moving *sefer* about the great mitzvah of lighting Shabbos candles. May the words of this book ignite Jewish women around the world to embrace this mitzvah, and to embrace the holy mission of spreading the light of Torah and the light of Shabbos, from our homes to the entire world.

With blessings,

Rabbi Warren Goldstein
Chief Rabbi of South Africa
Founder of The Shabbos Project

The Light of Shabbos

Shabbos – An Island of Peace

Each of the Jewish holidays appears on our calendars only once annually. The holy Shabbos, however, is a blessing we enjoy each and every week. The freshness and excitement of a once-yearly holiday helps us tap into its spiritual meaning and bounty, whereas the impact and importance of the weekly Shabbos may perhaps become a run-of-the-mill occurrence. How can we ensure that each and every Shabbos is truly an uplifting and inspiring occasion? We can answer this question by first defining Shabbos.

What is Shabbos? Succinctly put, Shabbos is our declaration and affirmation of our belief in Hashem. On Shabbos we do not work and do not effectuate any positive changes (*melachah*), as we place our destiny and relinquish all control into the Hands of Hashem, confident that He will care for all our needs. Shabbos is about coming to the realization that our abilities, successes, and profits issue from Hashem, and therefore, each Jew can feel: I can observe the Shabbos serenely, knowing that He is providing for me (see *Chorev*, Chapter 21).

In essence, Shabbos is our island of *emunah*, expressing our recognition of Hashem's absolute control of our lives. In an ever-pressurized environment that screams of egocentrism and man's ingenuity as being the sole source of his success, this affirmation is ever so important. More than 150 years ago, Rav Samson Raphael Hirsch wrote regarding society's view of life at the time: "The material world, the life around you, functions ceaselessly, never standing still, struggling endlessly, continuously moving forward. He who does not progress will regress, he who remains inactive will be trampled underfoot" (*Collected Writings,* Vol. 8, page 197). Shabbos is the time where we swim against the current of such thinking. We proudly stow away our tools, close our businesses, shut off our emails, and inculcate within ourselves that it is Hashem Who controls our jobs, accomplishments, and future.

Shabbos is the day of rest in which we revel in the absence of work pressure, shopping, and our ever-buzzing phones and emails. It is the one day a week where we can finally reconnect to our true selves and purposes. Shabbos presents the prime opportunity to disconnect from the world but reconnect to ourselves, our family, and God. Hashem calls out to each and every Jew, as he did to Adam in the Garden of Eden, "*Ayekah,* where are you?" Shabbos is the day for us to answer that call. Shabbos is an island of calm and peacefulness amid the stormy and distracting seas of our world. It is a barrier protecting that which is holy and precious.

And the Shabbos candles? They are like a lighthouse, illuminating and guiding us to the tranquil island of Shabbos.

Shabbos Candles and the Jewish Woman

Throughout our nation's miraculous history, the Shabbos has always remained the day the Jew has guarded ever so preciously, oftentimes incurring pain and humiliation in the process. Each generation has presented the Jew with overwhelming obstacles to his Shabbos observance, sometimes physical in nature and at times spiritual. Whether it was the Greeks, the Crusaders, the Spaniards, the Nazis, or the Communists, the Jew has steadfastly held on to his Shabbos, the pinnacle of Creation and the day of rest that defines his true identity. As even a non-observant thinker noted: "More than

the Jew has kept Shabbos, the Shabbos has kept the Jew."

For more than 4,000 years, Jewish women have devoutly fulfilled the mitzvah of lighting Shabbos candles, the mitzvah that ushers in the Shabbos and was first observed by our Matriarch Sarah. *Hadlakas neiros* is one of the three foundational mitzvos given specifically to women, and they have safeguarded this responsibility with utmost love and sacrifice regardless of the trying circumstances or their level of observance. The sight of a mother lighting her Shabbos candles is one that remains firmly imprinted onto the consciousness of her progeny, always reinforcing their awareness of the Shabbos and their Jewish identity.

The Inextinguishable Light

נֵר ה׳ נִשְׁמַת אָדָם

The candle of Hashem is the soul of man
(Mishlei 20:27)

*E*very single Jew has within him an inextinguishable Godly light. Just like a *shalheves,* flame, is always moving, the Jewish woman is continually in motion as she is involved in helping shape her home, her family, and all those with whom she comes in contact. With little rest, day in and day out, she is a source of light, warmth, and guidance to her family and the many that rely on her. Her spirit, efforts, energy, and the atmosphere of love and security that she injects into her home are ever vital to the continuity and preservation of the Godly light that exists within each of her progeny.

> *Shabbos candle lighting was a highlight of the week for Rebbetzin Batsheva Kanievsky. She would usually bring the Shabbos in early and would then sit opposite her candles with her hands covering her face, conversing with*

Hashem. It was at this time that the Rebbetzin would daven for her children, her family, and for those who had poured out their hearts to her in pain over the preceding week. The Rebbetzin would recite the names of hundreds of people and their specific needs without even looking at a paper. When asked how she could recall so many names, the Rebbetzin replied that each individual and his pain was etched into her heart, his pain was her pain and therefore it was of no difficulty to recall all of their names. At one point the Kanievsky home was being repainted and the area where the Rebbetzin's Shabbos candles were lit specifically required a fresh coat of paint. Yet her husband, Rav Chaim, told the Rebbetzin to please tell the painters not to paint the area of her Shabbos candles despite the fact that the wall was black and soot stained. Rav Chaim explained that the wall blackened from the special mitzvah of the Rebbetzin's hadlakas neiros is a most beautiful adornment and symbol for their home, one to be left for posterity and not removed (Rebbetzin Kanievsky, ArtScroll/Mesorah, page 206*).*

Hadlakas neiros is a highly auspicious time to pray for one's children, family, or any problem or challenge one faces. The onset of Shabbos, after the candles have been kindled, is a time when the doors of Heaven swing open, and all women need to do is to enter into this treasure house. Take these precious moments to bring up the faces of your children. Think about their struggles and needs and pray to Hashem. Know that your family and those that are close to you rely on your prayers that are ever so impactful to the success of their lives.

Remaining on the Island – Despite the Challenge

The name Rebbetzin Henny Machlis evokes a rush of love, warmth, and admiration to thousands of people around the globe. This Brooklyn-bred girl who settled in Eretz Yisrael with her husband Rabbi Mordechai had a crystal-clear vision for life: To use the Shabbos meal, her cooking, and her open home as a vehicle to bring fellow Jews, regardless of their religious background or appearance, closer to Hashem. A standard Shabbos in the Machlis home involved hosting anywhere between 50 and 150 people for each meal. Henny's warmth, her homemade food prepared and served with love, her absolute sensitivity and care for each guest, coupled with the lively and moving singing and divrei Torah, all contributed to the authentic, special Shabbos atmosphere in her home. This was the driving force motivating the thousands of souls who would return to the Machlis family again and again.

Sadly, at the age of 57, Henny succumbed to a terminal illness. Her family, her thousands of Shabbos guests, and the Jewish world mourned the loss of a holy woman. The seven days of mourning ended on a Thursday. On that very day, the Machlis family, sans their beloved wife and mother, perpetuated her legacy and immediately began cooking for their large contingent of Shabbos guests. The Friday-night meal began with an announcement from Rabbi Mordechai: "Shabbos," he said, "is an island of peace and joy. While each guest is asked to speak, I request that no one should deliver a message that can evoke sadness or grief." With unbelievable control and intense focus on the beauty of Shabbos, Rabbi Machlis beseeched his guests not to get swept into the sea of mourning and sorrow. "We have to stay on the island of Shabbos," he reminded them.

As per his instruction, the meal proceeded as

usual with merry singing, food, and divrei Torah. Then one of the regulars, an Oriental man who had arrived after Rabbi Machlis had made his request, rose to speak. Of course, he immediately began talking about Henny, tears flowing incessantly down his cheeks. Everyone turned toward Rabbi Mordechai to see if he would yield to his intense grief. Leib Yaacov Rigler, who was sitting next to Rabbi Machlis at the head of the table, urgently whispered, "Reb Mordechai, you're slipping off the island." At that moment, one of the guests began singing loudly, "Mitzvah gedolah l'hiyot b'simchah tamid, it is a great mitzvah to always be joyous." All of the men in the large crowd arose and, holding hands, their voices joined together in song. That Shabbos was a difficult Shabbos, no doubt, but the Machlis family and all their guests heroically and magically held their ground on the precious shores of the Shabbos island (Emunah with Love and Chicken Soup, ArtScroll/Mesorah, page 559).

May it be the Will of Hashem that each of us, no matter our challenges, worries, and difficulties of the week, merit to enter that peaceful island of Shabbos, an island that allows us to answer Hashem's call to each of us — "*Ayekah*, where are you?" — resolutely and with clarity: "*Hashem, I am with You!*"

Erev Shabbos Kodesh

לִקְרַאת שַׁבָּת לְכוּ וְנֵלְכָה כִּי הִיא מְקוֹר הַבְּרָכָה
To welcome the Shabbos come let us go, for it is the source of blessing

As day begins to turn into dusk and the soft shadows of the sun's last rays descend over the horizon, the time for candle lighting is here and Shabbos is ushered into the home. After a hectic day of preparations and anticipation, the moment arrives when the woman of the home at last stands at her candlesticks and lights the candles as serenity and peace descend upon her abode. Worries begin to dissipate and the ever-racing mind begins to slow and become more focused. Shabbos and its treasure house of blessings and tranquility is finally here.

Through observing the exalted day of Shabbos, we are rewarded with everlasting blessing. Shabbos is the source of all blessing, *ki hi mekor haberachah* (as the liturgical poem *Lechah Dodi* phrases it). The accepted time for lighting the Shabbos candles is 18 minutes before sunset. When we demonstrate our love for Shabbos by welcoming it in a timely manner, we are literally bestowing additional *berachah* into our lives. *Tosefes Shabbos* means that we take time from the weekday and transform it into the holiness of Shabbos. As we anxiously await the Shabbos and accept it punctiliously, it is likened to the special moment under the *chuppah* when the *chassan*-groom steps forward to greet his *kallah*-bride as she walks toward him (*Ohr HaChaim, Shemos* 31:16).

When Hashem introduced the commandment of observing the Shabbos to the Jewish nation, He instructed Moshe to tell the people, "I have a special gift in My treasure house and Shabbos is its name" (*Shabbos* 10b). What a gift we are privileged to accept! Ushering in the Shabbos in a timely manner is likened to having exclusive early access to a sale or a free giveaway. We tend to think that our profits from working during the week are reflective of the efforts and hours we expend. The truth is, though, that all successes we attain during the week are a direct result of the blessings bestowed by the holy Shabbos. Every moment of Shabbos is a gift delivered straight from the treasure house of Hashem, and each and every one of us can gain early access to this gift by accepting this holy day upon ourselves a bit early. These *berachos* can have a profound effect on our lives and the lives of our families. The *Zohar* (Vol. 2, 63b) writes that all successes gained during the entire six-day workweek stem from Shabbos. It is for this very reason the *Pri Megadim* (256:1) writes that one who accepts Shabbos early merits life.

The son-in-law of Rav Chaim Kanievsky, Rav Yitzchok Kolodetzky, writes that it is well known that Rav and Rebbetzin Kanievsky would encourage anyone who came to them with a dilemma, whether it involved health, finances, children, or *shidduchim,* to accept Shabbos upon themselves 10 minutes before the cited time of candle lighting. Rav Chaim would often explain, "It is within the power of accepting Shabbos early that one will merit children, health, financial stability, wealth, salvation from all pain and difficulty, a suitable marriage partner, and long life. The merit of accepting Shabbos early is immeasurable!" (*Tosefes Shabbos K'Hilchasah,* page 594).

On Shabbos Chol HaMoed Succos, in the recitation of the *Hoshanos* prayer, we recite: *Save us [in the merit] of those who hurry to bring in the Shabbos.* We are asking Hashem to grant us salvation in the merit of those who transform the *y'mei hachol,* the weekday, into the holiness of Shabbos.

Shabbos – The Healing Balm and Elixir of Life

We find that in times of great national or personal crisis Jews are called upon to take extra special care when performing the mitzvah of Shabbos candles. Since the Shabbos is the source of all blessing and is the day that nourishes the entire week with its bountiful *berachah,* its blessings are sought in times of distress and despair.

Mrs. Chaya Levine is a mother of nine and the widow of Rav Kalman, *Hy"d,* who was murdered on the dark day of November 18, 2014. He was cut down in the prime of life while in the Bnei Torah Shul located in Har Nof. Shortly after the tragic incident that took the lives of five great men, Mrs. Levine and several of the other widows of the martyrs gathered to speak words of *chizuk* to a large gathering of women in Yerushalayim. The following was her public request to the community: "I want to ask that we strengthen the observance of the three mitzvos that women are commanded to fulfill. The first is Shabbos candle lighting. No one knows better than me how busy we women are during the week and especially on Fridays. It is not uncommon that we are so exhausted as sunset approaches that we have no strength to think about the significance of the *berachah* we are about to recite. Therefore, I ask of you, from today forward, to please light candles 10 minutes earlier than the official time for candle lighting and take those extra minutes to think about *HaKadosh Baruch Hu* and to recite the *berachah* with *concentration*, with serenity and calm" (*Hamodia*, December 2, 2014).

After Rabbi Yonosan Sandler and his two young sons Aryeh and Gavriel were brutally murdered at their Otzar HaTorah School in Toulouse, France, the bereaved widow and mother, Chavah Sandler, was asked what people could do to provide her with consolation. She wrote, "Parents, please kiss your children. Tell them how much you love them, and how dear it is to your heart that they be living examples of our Torah, imbued with the fear of Heaven and love of their fellow man. Please bring more light into the world by kindling the Shabbos candles this and every Friday night … a bit earlier than the published times as a means of adding holiness and light to our world."

Please Protect the Shabbos

The sacred assignment of bringing Shabbos into our homes is a truly all-encompassing mitzvah with which women have been divinely entrusted. The way she handles her exalted role can not only influence her immediate family, but also generations to come. It is her energy, love, special food, attention to her children, and focus on Hashem that elevates her home into a palace, and her family into princes and princesses on this special day. The *pasuk* states (*Shemos* 31:16): וְשָׁמְרוּ בְנֵי יִשְׂרָאֵל אֶת הַשַּׁבָּת לַעֲשׂוֹת אֶת הַשַּׁבָּת לְדֹרֹתָם בְּרִית עוֹלָם, *The Children of Israel shall observe the Shabbos to make the Shabbos an eternal covenant for their generations.* Rav Shraga Feivel Mendelovitz explains that the Torah is telling us that Shabbos must be observed in such a way that it will be "for their generations" — perpetually loved and beloved by all future generations as well.

It is the mother, the *akeres habayis,* the backbone of her home, who can transform her home into a haven of calmness and holiness; who can focus on priorities even at the most hectic times of the week, on Erev Shabbos. This loving devotion and preparation for Shabbos is what will ensure that Shabbos is passed down to the future generations as well. It is the atmosphere and spirit of Shabbos, the sight of a mother standing in front of her Shabbos *neiros,* hands over eyes, silently praying for her family, that truly perpetuates the Shabbos.

Rabbi Yosef Dov Soloveitchik often recalled, "My father taught me *Mesechta Shabbos* whereas my mother taught me the beauty of Shabbos. Fathers teach their children how to observe Shabbos, mothers teach their children how to greet the Shabbos and to perceive her beauty and holiness." The aromas, smiles, shine, calmness, and general atmosphere of the home that the mother is charged with is what truly shapes and molds how Shabbos will be accepted each week. This tone and mood is what is remembered and replicated in subsequent generations.

Accepting Shabbos with Love

When we enter Shabbos calmly in our Shabbos attire we demonstrate our love, excitement, and respect for the arrival of the Shabbos Queen. Shabbos is a gift that Hashem gives to each of us individually. The way we stand at the Shabbos candles reflects how we view this gift. For this reason, the *sefarim* tell us that women should be dressed in their Shabbos finery upon lighting the candles since this is the momentous time when they are greeting the Shabbos, the gift from Hashem to each and every Jew (*M.B.* 262:11; *Avodas V'Hanhagos L'Beis Brisk,* Vol. 2, page 63).

In *tefillas Mussaf* of Shabbos we say: טוֹעֲמֶיהָ חַיִּים זָכוּ, *those who savor it will merit life.* Rabbi Zalman Sorotzkin explains that this is a reference to accepting Shabbos punctually. How does a wife know that her husband enjoyed the meal that she prepared for him? If he requests an additional portion he confirms his approval. Conversely, if he hardly touches the initial portion, let alone asks for more, she knows that the dish did not find favor in his eyes.

Hashem gave His children, the Jewish nation, a gift called Shabbos (*Shabbos* 10b). If we want to determine if this "gift" has found favor in someone's eyes, we can see how much of Shabbos she seeks.

Does she cut away at the gift, nonchalantly entering Shabbos at the last minute and dashing out of it at the first opportunity, or does she "take extras" by accepting the Shabbos early and delaying its departure? *To'ameha,* those who find the Shabbos sweet and precious and "take extras" by ushering it in early, *chaim zachu,* merit life and *berachah*! (*HaDei'ah V'HaDibur,* Vol. 3, 50:56).

Better One Less Cake for Shabbos

It is stated (*Mishlei* 15:17): טוֹב אֲרֻחַת יָרָק וְאַהֲבָה שָׁם מִשּׁוֹר אָבוּס וְשִׂנְאָה בוֹ, *Better a meal of greens where there is love than a fattened ox where there is hatred.* It states further (ibid. 17:1): טוֹב פַּת חֲרֵבָה וְשַׁלְוָה בָהּ מִבַּיִת מָלֵא זִבְחֵי רִיב, *Better a dry piece of bread and peace with it than a house full of celebrations that are quarrelsome.*

Sefer Chassidim (§863) understands these age-old dictums from Shlomo HaMelech to mean that even if one purchases special delicacies for Shabbos they are not worth anything if they come at the expense of peace in the home. What a crucial message! At times, on Erev Shabbos or late Thursday night, a wife may decide to bake something extra special for Shabbos or take upon herself an extra cleanup task. However, if time is short or it is late and she will be tired the next day, then tempers tend to be even shorter and this can result in anger and discord in the family. Of course, it is a special mitzvah to ensure that the Shabbos is brought in with a clean home and a table laden with food. But care needs to be taken that these activities do not infringe on the mother of the home's ability to enjoy the Shabbos and be a source of joy and light to her family.

Hashem prefers that there be one less cake, one less kugel, and one less dip for Shabbos as long as

there is *simchah* and peace in the home. Husbands and children would much prefer a mother who had gone to bed at a decent hour Thursday night or who was not harried the entire Friday even if that came at the expense of not having a homemade dessert. The Talmud (*Gittin* 52a) tells us that on Erev Shabbos the *yetzer hara* works extra diligently to create tension and conflict in the home. It wants us to come into Shabbos strained, disgruntled, and annoyed. This tactic is undertaken because it understands that Shabbos is the single oasis of time throughout the hectic week that we have to truly connect and bond with our families (*Matanah Tovah*, pages 19-21). Through the proper preparations, understanding our priorities and the importance of peace in the home, tension and conflict can be avoided.

Shabbos requires preparation no different than a wedding that needs to be planned well in advance. No mother is busy stuffing invitation envelopes the night before the *chuppah* of her daughter. Holiness requires preparation. The *pasuk* says: וְשָׁמְרוּ בְנֵי יִשְׂרָאֵל אֶת הַשַּׁבָּת, *and the Children of Israel shall observe the Shabbos*. The *Ohr HaChaim* (*Shemos* 31:16) explains that the word *V'shamru* can also mean "to anticipate." Only by anticipating and preparing for the Shabbos can a Jew properly tap into the bounty of blessing that is found on both Erev Shabbos and Shabbos.

What better *chinuch* can a mother provide her child than ushering in the Shabbos in a timely manner, with joy, involvement of the children, and with calmness? It is such an entrance into Shabbos that will instill in her children anticipation and a love for the holy day. The Talmud (*Shabbos* 119b) tells us that two angels, one good and one bad, accompany a man on his return home from shul Friday night. If upon his arrival home they see the Shabbos candles lit, the table set, and the home neat in honor of Shabbos, the good *malach* says, "May it be the Will [of Hashem] that it should be this way the next Shabbos as well," and the bad *malach* is forced to answer *Amen*. The woman of the home is the one who generally performs the lighting of the candles, setting of the table, and general preparation of the home in honor of Shabbos. It is these very acts and the hard work and efforts she invests that bring blessing into the home.

Giving Up Is Winning

One Erev Shabbos several hours before Shabbos, Rabbi Yoel Teitlebaum, the Satmar Rebbe, noticed his Rebbetzin setting up her Shabbos candles in the house. That week the Rebbe had been planning on conducting the meal-tisch in shul with all the chassidim. Whenever he did so, the custom was for the Rebbetzin to light Shabbos candles there. When the Rebbe asked the Rebbetzin why she was lighting at home, the Rebbetzin explained that due to his recent weakness she was not allowing him to strain himself to conduct the tisch that night. The chassidim, ever so eager to spend the Shabbos seudah with the Rebbe, would have to wait until he regained his strength. The Rebbe respectfully but firmly replied that he was feeling strong enough to conduct the tisch and that the Rebbetzin should prepare to light the Shabbos candles in the shul. The Rebbetzin held her ground and declared, "There will be no tisch tonight. The Rebbe and I will be eating home alone." Seeing his wife's concern for his health and her unshakeable resolve, the Rebbe acquiesced. Much to the chagrin of the chassidim, the tisch was canceled and the Rebbetzin would light the Shabbos candles at home.

A close student of the Rebbe who had witnessed the interchange between his Rebbe and the Rebbetzin was bewildered. How could it be that the Rebbe, known to be so unwavering and firm, would give in to his Rebbetzin just like that? Seeing his student's quizzical look, the Rebbe explained with a valuable and incisive pearl of wis-

dom: "You think that I lost the battle? I did not lose. On the contrary, I won. The one who gives in is the true winner!"

Throughout the entire week, but perhaps even more so on Erev Shabbos when the *yetzer hara* uses every weapon in its arsenal to create friction and discord in the home, relaxing our own personal rigidity and taking into account the feelings and experiences of another can be an awesome challenge. No one is denying its difficulty. But from the Shabbos candles, we learn a valuable lesson: A candle does not lose any of its light or brightness by lighting another candle. You never lose from giving in. You only burn brighter.

Charity Before Candle Lighting

There is a special custom for women to give *tzedakah* prior to lighting Shabbos candles. Why is this so? We know that a Jew's service of Hashem in this world is two-pronged but in essence fused as one. Both our relationship with Hashem and with our fellow man is of paramount and fundamental importance to the ideals the Torah embodies. The *Luchos* had two juxtaposed sides. The right side represents the mitzvos between man and God, and the left side represents the mitzvos between man and his fellow Jew. Yet, the *Luchos* were one. A Jew is complete in his service of God only if he strives to fulfill both his obligations to God and to his fellow man. One without the other is inherently flawed.

When we usher in the Shabbos, we light the Shabbos candles and pray that our children merit lighting the world with their Torah study and fear of Heaven. In our pursuit of welcoming the Shabbos, a proclamation and act that demonstrates our belief in

Hashem, we must make a special effort to fulfill our obligations toward our fellow man. Charity, making a phone call to one in need of encouragement, wishing family members a good Shabbos, sending a cake to a *simchah* or just as a means of conveying that you are thinking of another, are all vehicles to this end. They fuse the Shabbos that represents man's relationship with Hashem and the mitzvah of *bein adam la'chaveiro* (man's relationship with his fellow Jew) together to create an *adam hashaleim*, complete man.

The *Kitzur Shulchan Aruch* explains that candle lighting is a special time for *tefillah* and hence it is a propitious time to give charity, as the *pasuk* says (*Tehillim* 17:15): אֲנִי בְּצֶדֶק אֶחֱזֶה פָנֶיךָ, *I shall behold Your face through charity* (see *Shulchan Aruch* 92:10, where it states that it is meritorious to give charity prior to prayer).

Accepting Shabbos with a Chessed

Friday afternoon, the phone rang in the hospital room where the great Jewish leader Rabbi Moshe Feinstein lay ill. His son picked up the phone and asked the woman on the line if this was a life-threatening question for the great halachic sage. The caller was shocked. "Absolutely not, my question is not life threatening at all. I called the house and they told me the Rabbi is in the hospital so I called here."

"Well," said Rav Moshe's son, "the Rabbi is extremely weak and can barely speak. Please call back after Shabbos, perhaps my father will have more strength then."

"But my question is time sensitive and it cannot wait until after Shabbos!" the woman beseeched.

Hearing the panic in the woman's voice, Rav Moshe's son replied, "Okay, tell me the question

and I will ask my father."

A sigh of relief was breathed by the woman on the phone. "Please ask the Rabbi what time candle lighting is this week."

Rav Moshe's son was bewildered. For such a question the great leader lying sick in the hospital needed to be bothered? The woman explained, "Do you think that this is the first time I am calling Rav Moshe about this question? From the time that I became a widow I call Rav Moshe each and every week and he tells me the candle lighting time and blesses me with a good Shabbos!"

The same Rav Moshe whose every living moment was filled with learning Torah and answering halachic questions from around the world did not purchase a calendar with candle lighting times for this widow. Instead, Rav Moshe used this opportunity to encourage and provide solace to someone in need, a remarkable way of ushering in the Shabbos (ViHa'ish Moshe, Vol. 2, page 215).

The renowned Lady Amélie Jakobovits, wife of Lord Immanuel Jakobovits, Chief Rabbi of Great Britain, was a woman who showed acute care and concern for all. Hundreds of people considered her their best friend. At her funeral a son fondly told how one Erev Pesach, several years after the passing of their father, his mother made hundreds of phone calls to those so eagerly waiting for her blessing and words of encouragement.

We all are aware of people who can use some attention. Be it a grandparent, a relative, friends, a widow, a new neighbor in town, or a single, there is never a lack of people yearning for a warm human encounter. Shabbos can be a lonely time for many. Reaching out to these people on Erev Shabbos, even for just a brief call, can have an extraordinary effect on their Shabbos and the weeks to follow. There is nothing more special than ushering in Shabbos amid bringing joy to one who is in pain.

Candle Lighting

The Berachah, Impact, and Merits of Hadlakas Neiros Shabbos

Our Sages teach us the profound significance of lighting candles in honor of Shabbos.

- One who is careful and beautifies the mitzvah of *neiros Shabbos* will merit children who are Torah scholars. The *pasuk* (*Mishlei* 6:23): כִּי נֵר מִצְוָה וְתוֹרָה אוֹר, *for a commandment is a lamp and the Torah is light,* is homiletically interpreted to mean: *through the mitzvah of "ner" one will merit the light of Torah* (*Shabbos* 23b, *Rashi* ad loc.; *Tur* §263).

- Through lighting candles, women bequeath their husbands long life and, therefore, they must be meticulous that this mitzvah be performed with utmost care and concentration (*Zohar, Bereishis* 48b).

- In the merit of lighting Shabbos candles one will merit to see the lights of Tzion and Yerushalayim in the coming Redemption (*Yalkut Shimoni, Beha'aloscha* §719).

- The Shabbos candles place us under Hashem's protective shield so that the home is guarded and its atmosphere is infused with joy and peace (*Siduro Shel Shabbos, Shoresh* 2, 1:8).

- Hashem says to His people, the Jewish nation, "If you are careful to guard the mitzvah of *neiros* I will guard your *ner* [your *neshamah*, which is called a *ner*]" (*Shabbos* 32a).

- One who lights the Shabbos candles is as precious and dear to Hashem as Aharon the Kohen Gadol lighting the Menorah in the *Mishkan* (*Kedushas Levi, Chanukah* §3; *Igra D'Kallah, Parashas Tetzaveh*).

- It was due to the Jewish people's staunch adherence to the mitzvah of Shabbos candles that they merited to defeat the massive Greek armies and to find one remaining pure jug of oil to be used for the Menorah in the *Beis HaMikdash*. It was these events that were later commemorated as the holiday of Chanukah (*Kedushas Levi, Chanukah* §3; *Bnei Yissaschar, Kislev* 3:46).

Origins and Reasons for the Mitzvah of Lighting Candles on Erev Shabbos

❖ **Kavod Shabbos** — Lighting candles is a means of fulfilling the mitzvah of honoring the Shabbos and Yom Tov, a mitzvah derived from the *pasuk* (*Yeshayah* 58:13): לִקְדוֹשׁ ה׳ מְכֻבָּד, *[If you proclaim] … the holy [day] of Hashem "honored."* The presence of candles creates an aura of respect and importance, thereby adding to the prestige of Shabbos (*Shabbos* 24b; *Rambam, Shabbos* 30:5; see *Chinuch,* Mitzvah 98).

❖ **Shalom Bayis** — The presence of light prevents people from stumbling in the dark and becoming irritated with one another, thereby promoting peace and joy in the home. Peace and joy are an ever-integral component of Shabbos. There should be light in all rooms that one intends to enter on Shabbos (*Shabbos* 25b).

❖ **Oneg Shabbos** — Having light increases one's enjoyment of Shabbos and Yom Tov, as one can see and thereby enjoy his food. Someone stricken with visual impairment does not have the same pleasure from food as someone with full eyesight. Hence, one should ensure that the Shabbos candles will burn for the duration of the Friday-night meal (*Rambam* ibid. 5:1; *Shulchan Aruch* 263; *Kitzur Shulchan Aruch* 75:2).

Likewise, the Midrash (*Tanchuma, Noach* 1) sources the obligation to light Shabbos candles in the *pasuk* from the prophet Yeshayah

(58:13): וְקָרָאתָ לַשַּׁבָּת עֹנֶג, Proclaim the Shabbos "a delight."

* The Sadducees observed only the Written Torah (*Torah Shebiksav*) and not the Oral Torah. This misguided group opined that when the Torah writes (*Shemos* 35:3), לֹא תְבַעֲרוּ אֵשׁ בְּכֹל מֹשְׁבֹתֵיכֶם, *You shall not kindle fire in any of your dwellings [on the Sabbath day]*, it means that no light, whatsoever, shall be burning on Shabbos. However, the Talmud interprets the verse as a prohibition to kindle a light on Shabbos itself, but one may kindle a light prior to Shabbos. Hence, in order to dispel any notion of allegiance to the Sadducees we light candles prior to Shabbos to testify that we are staunch believers in the Oral Law of the Torah that permits fire to be kindled prior to Shabbos, even when the light will remain lit into Shabbos (*Sefer Chassidim* §1147; *Yalkut HaGershuni, Shulchan Aruch* 263:1; see *Ma'aseh Rav, Gra,* 114).

Selected Laws and Customs of Shabbos Candle Lighting

* Once a woman lights the Shabbos candles she has accepted Shabbos and may no longer perform any *melachah*, prohibited labor. Hence, all *melachah* must be completed before lighting the Shabbos candles. In unusual circumstances, where this is not feasible, a competent halachic authority should be consulted before the candles are lit.

* Women who are planning on *davening Minchah* should do so prior to lighting candles (*Mishnah Berurah* 263:43).

* It is the proper custom that women light the Shabbos candles dressed in their Shabbos finery, as it is at this point that they usher in the holiness of Shabbos. However, hastening to don Shabbos

clothing should not come at the expense of lighting candles on time (*Mishnah Berurah* 262:11; *Kaf HaChaim* 263:35).

❖ It is commendable for a woman to give charity prior to lighting candles (*Kitzur Shulchan Aruch* 72:2).

❖ In many communities, the man of the household prepares the Shabbos candles. Some have the custom that the man lights the candles and then extinguishes them (*Tosafos Rabbi Akiva Eiger, Shabbos* 2:6; *Mishnah Berurah* 264:28).

❖ One of the main functions of the Shabbos candles is to provide light for the Friday-night meal. Hence, the candles should be placed on or near the table where the meal will be eaten. If this is not feasible, one should consult a competent halachic authority (*Mishnah Berurah* 263:45).

❖ The generally accepted time for lighting the Shabbos candles is 18 minutes before sunset. If one delayed, the candles may be lit but one must ensure that they are kindled before *shkiah,* sunset. The custom in Jerusalem is to light Shabbos candles 40 minutes before sunset; some other communities have their own specific customs.

❖ The earliest one may accept Shabbos is from *plag haminchah* and onwards, which is one-and-a-quarter halachic hours before *shkiah* (sunset). One should consult a Jewish calendar for the proper time for their location and the specific date (*Mishnah Berurah* 263:19).

❖ If no candles are available, one should consult a competent halachic authority.

❖ One must benefit from the light of the Shabbos candles. It is preferable that the candles should burn for the entire duration of the Friday-night meal (*Kitzur Shulchan Aruch* 75:2; *Shemiras Shabbos K'Hilchasah* 43:17).

How Many Candles Should a Woman Light and Why?

❖ The prevailing custom is to light a minimum of two candles, one reflecting the mitzvah of *Zachor*, to remember and honor the Shabbos, and one reflecting *Shamor*, the mitzvah to safeguard the Shabbos and keep all its halachos (*Shulchan Aruch* 263:1).

❖ Additionally, the two candles are symbolic of the *neshamah yeseirah,* the extra *neshamah* with which one is gifted on Shabbos (*Mateh Moshe* §414).

❖ The two candles are also symbolic of a husband and wife. The numerical value of נר is 250 (נ=50, ר=200). Thus, the *gematria* of the words נר plus נר, symbolic of the two candles, is 500, which equals the total combined limbs of a man (248) and a woman (252) (*Elyah Rabbah* 263:2).

❖ In extenuating circumstances, a woman may fulfill her obligation by lighting only one candle (*Shulchan Aruch* 263:1).

❖ Many have the custom to add a candle upon the birth of each child, so that the additional light should serve as a merit that the child's Torah learning light up the world (*Likutei Maharich, Seder Hisnahagos Erev Shabbos*).

❖ Some have the custom to light seven candles, corresponding to a number of significant "sevens": the seven days of the week, the seven men called to the Torah on Shabbos, and the seven candles lit in the Menorah in the *Beis HaMikdash*. Others light ten candles corresponding to the Ten Commandments (*Ba'er Hateiv* 263:2; *Kaf HaChaim* 263:9).

❖ When a woman is not home for Shabbos or Yom Tov, the custom is that she lights only two candles, even if she lights more when she is at home (*Shemiras Shabbos K'Hilchasah,* Vol. 2, 43:3).

Candlesticks and Candles

The *Pele Yoetz* writes (*Ner Shabbos*): "It is well known that one who is careful with *neiros Shabbos* will merit children who are Torah scholars. 'Careful with this mitzvah' means that the candlestick one is lighting should be beautiful and clean, one should light with olive oil ... and if with all mitzvos one should make every effort to perform the commandment in the finest manner to bring joy to Hashem, then certainly [one should beautify] this mitzvah in which the reward (of children) is publicized, as one would give away all the money in his home so that his children merit the crown of Torah."

Many have the custom to light with olive oil, as oil burns the brightest (*Shulchan Aruch* 264:6). Nevertheless, nowadays, where our wax and paraffin candles burn efficiently and produce a bright flame, many have the custom to light with these. One should follow her respective family custom (*Mishnah Berurah* 264:23).

As to why specifically olive oil is the fuel of choice for many, the Talmud tells us that one who lights candles merits children who are Torah scholars, and the Talmud compares the Torah scholar to olive oil (*Machzik Berachah*). *Sefer Chassidim* (272) tells of a person who lived a very long life and they found the only extra merit he had was that he lit the Shabbos candles with olive oil. The Talmud (*Shabbos* 23b) blesses one who is careful to light Shabbos candles that she will merit children who are Torah scholars. Some learn that this blessing is conferred on those who light with olive oil (*Eishel Avraham* 263:1; *Machzik Berachah* 264:2).

The *Midrash Chadash* (page 257) writes that olive oil is unique in that it separates itself from the liquids that surround it and rises to the top. So too as long as the Jewish people separate and distinguish themselves from the non-Jewish ideals and practices that surround them they will merit to rise to the top (see *Shir HaShirim Rabbah* 1:3).

Why Was the Mitzvah of Lighting Shabbos Candles Given Specifically to Women?

Although both men and women are obligated in the mitzvah of *hadlakas neiros*, women were granted priority in the performance of this mitzvah. Why is this so?

❖ When Chavah convinced Adam to eat from the *Eitz HaDa'as*, the Tree of Knowledge, Hashem decreed that mankind would no longer live forever; death was introduced to the world. The soul of a person is compared to a candle — נֵר ה׳ נִשְׁמַת אָדָם (*Mishlei* 20:27). As a means of attaining forgiveness for Chavah "extinguishing the candle of the world," Jewish women throughout the generations light candles on the eve of Shabbos (*Tur* §263).

❖ Additionally, the sin of Chavah, her convincing Adam to partake of the fruit, and the subsequent punishments handed down by Hashem undoubtedly created tension between her and her husband Adam. It is for this reason that women light the Shabbos candles, whose essence is to provide light in the home, thereby preventing all of the divisiveness and discord that can result from a home shrouded in darkness.

Every mitzvah brings light into the world and conversely every sin brings darkness into the world. When Chavah convinced Adam to eat from the *Eitz HaDa'as* a sin was committed and darkness was introduced to the world. As a means of banishing this darkness and bringing additional light into the world, the mitzvah of lighting Shabbos candles was given to women.

Death is the physical expiration of the body and was introduced by Chavah's sin. On the other hand, man's spiritual accomplishments, such as his Torah and mitzvah achievements, live on forever, unaffected by the punishment of her sin. The *pasuk* says: כִּי נֵר מִצְוָה וְתוֹרָה אוֹר, *for a commandment is a lamp and the Torah is light* (*Mishlei* 6:23). Although Chavah's sin brought physical death to the world, and this cannot be changed, women light Shabbos candles and pray that their families' spiritual and eternal life merit lighting up the world for all eternity.

❖ It is the women who are generally in the home and are primarily responsible for its smooth functioning. They therefore merit performing the mitzvah of *hadlakos neiros,* thereby ensuring there will be ample light and harmony in the home (*Shulchan Aruch* 263:3).

❖ The Torah refers to Jewish women as the *Beis Yaakov,* House of Yaakov. In addition to meaning *home,* the word *bayis* also means *inside.* A home is private and safe; it is protected and is not exposed to the world at large. While the husband's responsibilities usually cause him to be out of the home, the wife is charged with instilling the four walls of her home with Torah values, spirit, and love. It is the women who define and mold the atmosphere of their homes, assuring that their families feel secure, content, and loved.

There are two mitzvos that involve lighting candles: kindling the Chanukah lights and lighting the Shabbos candles. While men and women are obligated to fulfill both mitzvos, when it comes to lighting Chanukah candles — which are placed outside or at a window to shine their light to the **outside** world — women defer the lighting to the man of the house. However, regarding the lighting of the Shabbos candles — which are lit inside and whose essence is to infuse the **inside** of the home with peace and serenity – men defer to the women, the *Beis Yaakov,* the inner foundation, the energy and inspiration of the Jewish home, to kindle the holy Shabbos candles (*Selected Writings of Rav Shimon Schwab,* page 327).

Hadlakas Neiros

On the eve of Shabbos, the candles are lit, the match or lighter placed down, and the eyes are covered with one's hands. Many women wave their hands in front of the candles (some do so three times) before covering the face.
The following berachah is then recited.:

בָּרוּךְ אַתָּה יהוה אֱלֹהֵינוּ מֶלֶךְ הָעוֹלָם, אֲשֶׁר קִדְּשָׁנוּ בְּמִצְוֹתָיו, וְצִוָּנוּ לְהַדְלִיק נֵר שֶׁל שַׁבָּת.

BORUCH ATO ADONOY ELOHAYNU MELECH HO-ŌLOM, ASHER KID'SHONU B'MITZVOSOV, V'TZIVONU L'HADLIK NAYR SHEL SHABOS.

Blessed are You, Hashem, our God, King of the universe, Who has sanctified us with His commandments, and has commanded us to kindle the light of the Sabbath.

Some have the custom to recite the following:

יְהִי רָצוֹן מִלְּפָנֶיךָ, יהוה אֱלֹהֵינוּ וֵאלֹהֵי אֲבוֹתֵינוּ, שֶׁיִּבָּנֶה בֵּית הַמִּקְדָּשׁ בִּמְהֵרָה בְיָמֵינוּ, וְתֵן חֶלְקֵנוּ בְּתוֹרָתֶךָ. וְשָׁם נַעֲבָדְךָ בְּיִרְאָה, כִּימֵי עוֹלָם וּכְשָׁנִים קַדְמוֹנִיּוֹת. וְעָרְבָה לַיהוה מִנְחַת יְהוּדָה וִירוּשָׁלָיִם, כִּימֵי עוֹלָם וּכְשָׁנִים קַדְמוֹנִיּוֹת.

Y'HI ROTZŌN MIL'FONECHO, ADŌNOY ELŌHAYNU VAYLŌHAY AVŌSAYNU, SHE-YIBO-NE BAYS HAMIKDOSH BIMHAYRO V'YOMAYNU, V'SAYN CHELKAYNU B'SŌ-ROSECHO, V'SHOM NA-AVOD-CHO B'YIRO, KIMAY ŌLOM UCHSHONIM KADMŌNIYŌS. V'OR'VO LADŌNOY MINCHAS Y'HUDO VIRUSHOLO-YIM KIMAY ŌLOM UCHSHONIM KADMŌNIYŌS.

May it be Your will, Hashem, our God and God of our forefathers, that the Holy Temple be rebuilt, speedily in our days. Grant us our share in Your Torah, and may we serve You there with reverence, as in days of old and in former years. Then the offering of Judah and Jerusalem will be pleasing to Hashem, as in days of old and in former years.

Candle Lighting — 45

With the lighting of the candles, it is a highly auspicious time for prayer and the following *tefillah* is customarily recited:

יְהִי רָצוֹן לְפָנֶיךָ, יהוה אֱלֹהַי וֵאלֹהֵי אֲבוֹתַי, שֶׁתְּחוֹנֵן אוֹתִי [וְאֶת אִישִׁי, וְאֶת בָּנַי, וְאֶת בְּנוֹתַי, וְאֶת אָבִי, וְאֶת אִמִּי] וְאֶת כָּל קְרוֹבַי; וְתִתֶּן לָנוּ וּלְכָל יִשְׂרָאֵל חַיִּים טוֹבִים וַאֲרוּכִים; וְתִזְכְּרֵנוּ בְּזִכְרוֹן טוֹבָה וּבְרָכָה; וְתִפְקְדֵנוּ בִּפְקֻדַּת יְשׁוּעָה וְרַחֲמִים; וּתְבָרְכֵנוּ בְּרָכוֹת גְּדוֹלוֹת; וְתַשְׁלִים בָּתֵּינוּ; וְתַשְׁכֵּן שְׁכִינָתְךָ בֵּינֵינוּ. וְזַכֵּנִי לְגַדֵּל בָּנִים וּבְנֵי בָנִים חֲכָמִים וּנְבוֹנִים, אוֹהֲבֵי יהוה, יִרְאֵי אֱלֹהִים, אַנְשֵׁי אֱמֶת, זֶרַע קֹדֶשׁ, בַּיהוה דְּבֵקִים, וּמְאִירִים אֶת הָעוֹלָם בַּתּוֹרָה וּבְמַעֲשִׂים טוֹבִים, וּבְכָל מְלֶאכֶת עֲבוֹדַת הַבּוֹרֵא. אָנָּא שְׁמַע אֶת תְּחִנָּתִי בָּעֵת הַזֹּאת, בִּזְכוּת שָׂרָה וְרִבְקָה וְרָחֵל וְלֵאָה אִמּוֹתֵינוּ, וְהָאֵר נֵרֵנוּ שֶׁלֹּא יִכְבֶּה לְעוֹלָם וָעֶד, וְהָאֵר פָּנֶיךָ וְנִוָּשֵׁעָה. אָמֵן.

Y'HI RATZON L'FONECHO, ADONOY ELOHAI VAYLOHAY AVOSAI, SHET'CHONAYN OSI [V'ES ISHI, V'ES BONAI, V'ES B'NOSAI, V'ES OVI, V'ES IMI] V'ES KOL K'ROVAI, V'SITEN LONU ULCHOL YISRO-AYL CHAYIM TOVIM VA-ARUCHIM, V'SIZK'RAYNU B'ZICHRON TOVO UVROCHO, V'SIFK'DAYNU BIFKUDASNY'SHU-O V'RACHAMIM, USVOR'CHAYNU B'ROCHOS G'DOLOS, V'SASHLIM BOTAYNU, V'SASHKAYN SH'CHINOS'CHO BAYNAYNU, V'ZAKAYNI L'GADAYL BONIM UVNAY VONIM CHACHOMIM UNVONIM, OHAVAY ADONOY, YIR-AY ELOHIM, ANSHAY EMES, ZERA KODESH, BADONOY D'VAYKIM, UM-IRIM ES HO-Ō-LOM BATORO UVMA-ASIM TOVIM, UVCHOL M'LECHES AVODAS HABORAY. ONO SH'MA ES T'CHINOSI BO-AYS HAZOS, BIZCHUS SORO, V'RIVKO, V'ROCHAYL V'LAYO I-MOSAYNU, V'HO-AYR NAYRAYNU SHELO YICHBE L'OLAM VO-ED, V'HO-AYR PONECHO V'NIVOSHAY-O. OMAYN.

May it be Your will, Hashem, my God and God of my forefathers, that You show favor to me [my husband, my sons, my daughters, my father, my mother] and all my relatives; and that You grant us and all Israel a good and long life; that You remember us with a beneficent memory and blessing; that You consider us with a consideration of salvation and compassion; that You bless us with great blessings; that You make our households complete; that You cause Your Presence to dwell among us. Privilege me to raise children and grandchildren who are wise and understanding, who love Hashem and fear God, people of truth, holy offspring, attached to Hashem, who illuminate the world with Torah and good deeds and with every labor in the service of the Creator. Please, hear my plea at this time, in the merit of Sarah, Rivkah, Rachel, and Leah, our mothers, and cause our light to illuminate that it not be extinguished forever, and let Your countenance shine so that we are saved. Amen.

The *Shelah* notes that is meritorious for women to recite the Haftarah of the first day of Rosh Hashanah; see page 69.

Once the candles are kindled, why are the eyes covered before the blessing is recited?

Ordinarily, a *berachah* is recited prior to the performance of the mitzvah. Yet, the instance of *hadlakas neiros* and its blessing is unique. If the blessing on the Shabbos candles would be recited first this would constitute an acceptance of the Shabbos and it would be forbidden to then kindle the Shabbos candles. In order to satisfy all halachic concerns, the candles are lit first, the eyes are covered so as not to benefit from the light, the *berachah* is then recited, and the eyes uncovered so that only then does one benefit from the candles. It is thus as if the blessing preceded the mitzvah.

Illuminate the World

The Eternity of the Shabbos Candles

In the mid-1990's a Jewish outreach professional envisioned that having the New York City candle lighting times for each Shabbos printed on the front page of the prestigious *New York Times* Friday edition would create a profound awareness of Shabbos. A well-known philanthropist sponsored the $2,000 per week ad. As a result, in every Friday edition of the *Times* there appeared a small box at the bottom left corner of the front page with that week's candle lighting times for New York City. The ad appeared for five years straight. There then came a time that the philanthropist was unable to continue his donations toward the project and the candle lighting ad ceased to appear in the *Times*. Many assumed that this ad would never be seen again.

On January 1, 2000, the new millennium was ushered in and *The New York Times* printed three editions of the paper that day. One was the actual news for January 1, 2000. The second was a reprint of *The New York Times* from the year 1900 — 100 years earlier. The third was a January 1, 2100 edition with news of what the paper's journalists speculated would be taking place 100 years in the future. On the front cover of the 2100 edition was a small, familiar box — the candle lighting time for New York for Friday, January 1, 2100. Who had requested that this be placed there? Who had paid for this? The production manager for the *Times*, an Irish Catholic, was asked for an explanation and he related, "No one knows what the world will be like in the year 2100. We cannot predict the future, but one thing we can be assured of, and that is that on Friday afternoon, January 1, 2100, Jewish women will be lighting the Shabbos candles" (*Peninim Al HaTorah,* Vol. 21, page 120).

From our Matriarch Sarah through the most challenging times in our history, Jewish women, regardless of their level of observance, have sacrificed for this special mitzvah. They have ensured that the spark and flame of Judaism and the Shabbos ignites and warms its adherents until today. It is the Shabbos and the Jew that has withstood the test of time. The "isms" have all but vanished with only Judaism and the Torah dispersing light onto the Jewish nation. It is the *Ner Mitzvah V'Torah Ohr,* the light of the Torah and mitzvah observance, that have provided us a guiding light in an often dark, challenging, and unpredictable world.

The Shabbos Candles that Burned All Week

The Midrash (*Parashas Chayei Sarah* 60:16) writes that as long as Sarah was alive the Presence of Hashem rested above her home, her doors were open wide to guests, her bread was blessed, and the light from her Shabbos candles burned continuously from Erev Shabbos to Erev Shabbos. When Sarah passed away these four blessings ceased and only returned once Yitzchak brought Rivkah into their home as his wife. Rav Samson Raphael Hirsch gleans from here that the Presence and blessings of Hashem and the atmosphere of *chessed* and tranquility in the home are all direct products of the women residing within it (*Collected Writings of Rav Hirsch,* Vol. 8, page 102).

The Talmud (*Shabbos* 118b) tells us that Rav Yose would refer to his wife as his "home," since it is the wife who sets the atmosphere in the home that shapes and molds the family to live a life of Torah and mitzvos. Rabbi Aryeh Levin was once traveling by taxi, and the driver asked him where his home was located. Rav Aryeh paused and then

said, "From the day that my wife died I do not have a home; I have a street address, but not a home" (*HaMashgiach D'Kaminetz,* page 223).

What is the message that we are to take away from Sarah's and Rivkah's Shabbos candles remaining lit from Shabbos to Shabbos? Rav Shimshon Pincus explains that the illuminating Shabbos candles infuse the home with peace. Holy women such as the Matriarchs made every effort to ensure that their homes were an oasis of peace, tranquility, and harmony — not only on Shabbos, when people are less harried, but even throughout the entire week, when people are so busy and even the slightest mishap can result in tension and anger. This was reflected in their Shabbos candles that miraculously remained lit, providing an aura of serenity and *shalom bayis* throughout the entire week. It is the women of the home, with their spirit, emotion, and warmth, who can create a happy, peaceful, secure, and warm home for their family. Such a home will exude a continual light like the light that emanated from the tents of our Matriarchs (*Tiferes Shimshon, Bereishis,* page 254).

It is a nearly universal custom that in all homes, *Eishes Chayil* (*Mishlei* 31:10-31) is recited immediately prior to the start of the Friday-night Shabbos meal. In a twenty-two-stanza praise of the Jewish woman that follows the letters of the Hebrew alphabet, the Jewish wife is lauded for her sacrifice, love, noble spirit, and dedication to her family and home. How apropos it is that at this special time, with the family gathered around the table, the home shining with Shabbos, and the culmination of her hard work at hand, the family joins together in the *Eishes Chayil* song praising their hardworking wife and mother for all she does in creating and shaping her home.

From Darkness to Light

That Friday afternoon many already knew of their coming fate. Inhumanely packed into the Nazi transport train, the starving, freezing, and beaten occupants could only sink further into their misery as the train rolled endlessly on toward a location that only portended the worst.

Suddenly, as the sun began to set, an elderly woman reached into her small satchel and removed two candlesticks and two challos. As she was mercilessly dragged from her home that morning they were the only two items she found worthwhile taking with her. The Shabbos candles were then lit and their warm and ever-familiar light illuminated and uplifted the faces and spirits of the broken Jews as the song of Lechah Dodi welcoming the Shabbos filled the train car. The Shabbos had descended upon them, transforming the depressed and hopeless atmosphere into one of serenity and belief. Such is the transformative nature of the Shabbos and its candles (The Sabbath, Dayan Grunfeld, Feldheim Publ., page 13).

Rabbi Yaakov Bender, Rosh Yeshivah of Yeshivah Darchei Torah, was approached by a middle-aged woman who wished to divulge a personal story about Rabbi Bender's mother, Rebbetzin Basya Bender:

> *It was Friday afternoon during the shivah for my first husband who had passed away suddenly as a young man. The house was empty, as those who usually would be offering comfort were busy preparing for Shabbos, and I sat there on a low stool terribly depressed and overtaken by my morbid thoughts. Then there was a knock on the door and in walked your mother, Rebbetzin Bender, and these were the words she comforted me with:*
>
> *"I am all too familiar with the pain you are enduring now because my husband also passed away in his prime leaving behind me and our*

children. The first Friday-night meal without my husband was particularly difficult. We gathered around our seats but when we saw my husband's empty place at the head of the table we all burst into tears.

"It is but a short time before Shabbos arrives, and therefore, please heed my advice: Before Shabbos, take your tray with the Shabbos candles and place it at the head of the table right in front of your husband's place and light the candles there. This way, whenever you longingly look at your husband's missing presence at the table your eyes will see the Shabbos candles and you will draw strength from their holy glow."

Although that first Friday night was not an easy one, I followed your mother's suggestion and I was glad that I had. The light of the Shabbos candles was a healing balm for our broken spirits (Living the Parashah, Vol. 3, page 230).

Shabbos Candles and Shalom Bayis

The rebbi of the Chafetz Chaim, Rav Nachum'ke of Horodna, was a man of extraordinary character and steadfast devotion to even the minutest detail of halachah. On the first night of Chanukah, the Chafetz Chaim went to observe how his rebbi performed the mitzvah of neiros Chanukah, and positioned himself across the street to gain a favorable vantage point. The time for lighting candles came and passed. The Chafetz Chaim was perplexed in that there was no sign of Rav Nachum'ke at his window. After waiting three hours, Rav Nachum'ke was finally seen at his window lighting the Chanukah candles.

The Chafetz Chaim was bewildered. His rebbi was so scrupulous when it came to mitzvos, yet here the rebbi lit three hours after the optimal *time for lighting. What could be the explanation for this? Having a burning desire to understand his rebbi's ways, the Chafetz Chaim knocked on the door and apologized for his imprudence, respectfully inquiring as to why the rebbi lit so late.*

Rav Nachum'ke explained, "The Talmud (Shabbos 23b) tells us that if one has only enough money to purchase Chanukah candles or Shabbos candles, Shabbos candles take precedence, as their purpose is to provide shalom bayis, the vital peace in the home. Tonight my wife returned late from a trip. Had I not waited for her and lit the Chanukah neiros at their optimal time, undoubtedly she would have been disappointed. The Talmud teaches us neiros Shabbos, which infuses the home with shalom bayis, take precedence over neiros Chanukah. Therefore, in order to ensure that there was harmony in my home I waited for my wife to light the Chanukah candles" (She'al Avicha V'yagedcha, Vol. 3, page 197).

The mitzvah of *neiros Chanukah* is *pirsumei nisa*, to publicize the great miracles Hashem performed on behalf of the Jewish people. This mitzvah is so great that one is obligated to go door-to-door soliciting alms in order to purchase candles. Yet *neiros Shabbos*, whose purpose is to instill peace within the home, takes precedence! The Presence of Hashem dwells in a home of peace and harmony. More important than publicizing the Godly Powers of Hashem to the masses is ensuring that in one's very own home there is peace and that the Presence of Hashem can be found. Often, we assume that our mitzvos and acts of *chessed* accomplished outside the home are more prized than our mitzvos and acts of goodwill performed within the home. The priority given by Rav Nachum'ke to peace in the home clearly relays to us how Hashem treasures a home of love and harmony where He can rest His Presence.

A light can remain burning only if one tends to the fire by constantly adding oil and ensuring the wick is properly placed. Left alone without additional involvement and oil the flame will eventually

dim and flicker out. The connection between the Shabbos candles and *shalom bayis* internalizes the message that marriage likewise cannot operate on a cruise control setting. Similar to a fire it requires constant tending and work to keep it aflame. Seeking to drive home this ever-vital message, the famed Mashgiach Rav Yechezkiel Levenstein approached a newly married student of his and asked, "What did you do **today** for your *shalom bayis*?"

Me, You, and Us – The Lesson of the Candles

Upon marriage, one prevalent custom is for the wife to light two Shabbos candles each week and subsequently add a candle for each child born. Some explain that these two candles, whose purpose is to bring light and peace into the home, are symbolic of husband and wife (*Mateh Moshe,* Vol. 4 §414). The Hebrew word for one's face is *panim*. The word *panim* also means "inside." It is noted that the human face, with its varied expressions and ever-expressive eyes, are the ultimate revealer of one's emotional status. The face is a tell-all of what is occurring inside one's soul — his *penimiyus*. In the absence of light, the face cannot be seen and one cannot perceive his fellow man's emotions, sensitivities, and state of mind. Light changes all of this. With light we can distinguish our fellow man's state of mind and act accordingly, thereby promoting peace and friendship.

Although each of the two Shabbos candles is distinct and has its own fuel source, wick, and flame, their illumination fuses and harmonizes to form one bright light. Marriage is not about each spouse abandoning their individuality and preferences while forming a new entity called "us." Rather, it is about taking the "me" — my uniqueness — and the "you" — your special qualities that only you bring into this world — and working together in order to generate a single light for our home and family. Marriage is about two distinct people, each with various strengths and weaknesses, who make a commitment to become better people through complementing each other's traits.

Rav Yaakov Galinsky summed it up ever so succinctly: Two people with strikingly similar character traits and personalities who choose to get married would be similar to wearing two left shoes. A successful marriage is one right shoe and one left shoe. It is a husband and wife deploying their differences and uniqueness as a means of effectively complementing those of their mate and developing a healthy marriage and home that shines with one bright light.

The Penetrating Message of the Shabbos Candles

As a young graduate student at the Tel Aviv University, Jeffrey had been brought up with limited exposure to Judaism and its meanings. From time to time he would meet with a young rabbi from the neighboring city of Bnei Brak and discuss various principles of Judaism, its ideals, and the wisdom of the Torah. Jeffrey's study partner would invite him for a Shabbos meal but Jeffrey always turned down the offer, apprehensive of crossing the border into the world of the Shabbos observer.

After some time, Jeffrey's apprehensiveness began to diminish and he finally accepted his study partner's invitation for that coming Friday night meal. After the Friday night prayer service, Jeffrey and his host walked home and upon opening the front door were unpleasantly met with darkness. It seems that an electrical fault had cut the electricity in the entire home and aside from the soft glow of the Shabbos candles in the dining room the house was cloaked in darkness. Jeffrey's host was understandably concerned that the darkened home would taint Jeffrey's impression of the Shabbos. After apologizing and

explaining why the lights could not be turned back on, the host recited Kiddush by the warm glow of the Shabbos candles, and the meal continued amidst delicious homemade food, merry singing, the children answering parashah questions, and enlightening words of Torah.

Even after the meal, Jeffrey and his host continued talking until well past midnight. Eventually, as the hour was late the discussion wound down and Jeffrey's host escorted him to the door. Jeffrey thanked his host for a beautiful and inspiring night, the likes of which he had never experienced before. "But one thing truly left an indelible mark on me," added Jeffrey. "We live in a technologically advanced era in which for even our most basic needs we are dependent on the innovations and advancements that modernity has introduced. I saw here tonight in your home that one can enjoy a life full of meaning and serenity without relying on technology. As we sat by the light of the ancient Shabbos candles I felt I was transported to a different world, a world of freedom and truth. A thousand hours of talking about the importance of Shabbos could not have provided me with the appreciation and feelings that this one meal, illuminated with only the light of the Shabbos candles, have instilled within me" (The Sabbath, Dayan Grunfeld, Feldheim Publ., page 80).

Seeing Is Tasting

*C*hida and others cite an enigmatic Midrash that cites the *pasuk* describing the complaints of the Jewish nation in the Wilderness regarding the *manna* (Bamidbar 11:5): זָכַרְנוּ אֶת הַדָּגָה מִכָּאן שֶׁמַּדְלִיקִין נֵרוֹת שַׁבָּת, "'*We remember the fish [that we ate in Egypt]*' — from here we learn to light Shabbos *neiros*." What is the connection between the Jewish people longing for fish and an obligation to light Shabbos candles?

In order to answer this, we need to understand why the Jewish people had a longing for fish — were they not eating from the *manna* that had the taste of any dish they desired? The answer to this is that although the *manna* had any given desired taste, it always had the same appearance and did not take the appearance of the food that it tasted like. The Jewish people longingly recalled the **sight** of the fish and of other foods that the *manna* could not provide. From here we see the considerable enjoyment that comes along with visually seeing one's food, and hence there is a mitzvah to have light at the Shabbos table so as to enjoy one's food (*Ta'amei HaMinhagim,* page 124).

The Light of Creation, the Light of the Shabbos Candles

On Day One of Creation, when the world was astonishingly empty and dark, the very first entity Hashem fashioned was light. The creation of light is the very opening testament and affirmation of a Godly Presence forming and sustaining this world. Simply stated, light is a beacon of *emunah* in Hashem. The essence of Shabbos observance is pure belief in Hashem: belief that He created the world in six days and rested on the seventh; belief that He will care for me and all my needs despite the fact that I will not be working on this day. It is for this very reason that the Shabbos is brought in with light, the very creation that introduced Hashem's Presence to the world.

The Talmud (*Taanis* 25a) relates that one Erev Shabbos, R' Chanina ben Dosa noticed that his daughter was clearly saddened. "What happened, my daughter, why are you so gloomy?" asked Rav Chanina. His daughter, who had just kindled the Shabbos candles, explained, "I accidently mistook a container of vinegar for a container of oil. In just moments the candles will extinguish, leaving us

here in the dark." Rav Chanina calmed his daughter, "What does it matter to you? The One Who commanded oil to burn can command vinegar to burn as well." That Shabbos the candles burned throughout the entire day and they were able to use their flame for *Havdalah* as well. This account of Rav Chanina ben Dosa and his daughter affirms to each of us that even the most basic laws of nature are all the products of Hashem's Will, the Designer of the world, and can be altered at His wish.

It may be for this reason that the *Rama* (*Orach Chaim* 271:10) tells us that when one begins the Friday-night *Kiddush* recitation it is meritorious to gaze at the Shabbos candles. *Kiddush* proclaims for all to hear that God created the world in six days, with the seventh day, the Shabbos, serving as the culmination and climax of Creation. Is there a more apropos time to peer at the Shabbos candles, the very first creation, than at the start of the *Kiddush*?

When standing in front of the Shabbos candles, look at the flames and internalize that this light was the very first creation here on earth. It is this light that strengthens my belief in the Creator of the world, in the One Who is watching over me with Divine Intervention. Coupled with our selfless observance of the Shabbos, a testament of our belief in Hashem, He should bestow upon us the blessings of those who believe and trust in Him: בָּרוּךְ הַגֶּבֶר אֲשֶׁר יִבְטַח בַּה׳ וְהָיָה ה׳ מִבְטַחוֹ, *Blessed is the man who trusts in Hashem, then Hashem will be his security* (*Yirmiyah* 17:7).

Every Child Brings into the Home and the World a Special Light

Many have the custom to light an additional candle for every child born into the family. Rabbi Avraham J. Twerski explains that the presence of every additional candle brings more light into the home. The message to our children is no matter who you are, what your grades are, or how you behave, Mommy lights a candle for you because you bring brightness and joy into this home and into the world. In today's world, where feelings of inadequacy and inferiority are all too common, this message that every child's Shabbos candle brings a unique light into the home and the world is ever so important and illuminating (*Generation to Generation,* page 75).

Light Amidst the Dark

During the Holocaust, the Nazis did everything in their power to both physically and spiritually exterminate the Jewish people and sever their adherence to mitzvos. Those who were not shot, starved, or gassed suffered indescribable tortures and were forbidden to perform any form of mitzvah observance. Those caught laying *tefillin,* keeping Shabbos, or blowing a shofar were shot immediately. Yet, the Jewish nation is not one to part from its precious mitzvos. The *sefarim* write (see *Kedushas Levi, Parashas Vayeira* 22:12) that the word mitzvah comes from the word "*tzavsa*" which means "together." Mitzvos are a vehicle that bring us close to Hashem. It was the unbelievable steadfast dedication to mitzvos of so many Jews at this time that strengthened their bond with Hashem. It was this connection that was so integral to their emotional stability that many survivors pinpointed as their guiding light, and that ignited their ability to survive the harshest of conditions.

One survivor, Na'ami Winkler, tells how she and her friends attempted to create light amid the darkest of times:

> "We made every effort to usher in the spirit of the holy Shabbos each week through lighting candles and reciting the prayers of Shabbos. Throughout all of our afflicted travels [from camp to camp] we tried our best to light the Shabbos and Yom Tov candles. At times, we took a potato, made a small

hole in it, lined it with margarine, and used threads from our clothing as a wick. When we worked in a gun factory, we would smuggle small bolts to use as candle holders and fill them with grease from the machinery as oil. We were constantly employing innovative methods to assure that we would have the means of lighting Shabbos candles.

"Yet, there were times when there was just nothing to light candles with. Still, our spirits were not broken. I still recall how on a dark Friday afternoon in November 1944 we were marching in rows of five on our way to a twelve-hour night-labor shift. Our clothing was torn and the march was treacherous and long. All of a sudden the girl next to me said, 'Now I just lit the Shabbos candles.' I waited for her to provide an explanation as there were no candles in sight. She explained, 'We just passed two street lamps and I recited the berachah of the Shabbos neiros over them.' What dominated the thoughts of Jewish women at a time of immense and prolonged suffering, years of torture, starvation, and deplorable subhuman conditions? How can we fulfill the mitzvah of Shabbos candles" (Zachor, Vol. 10, page 68).

When you stand by the Shabbos candles, understand how vital you are in the link of the Jewish nation's remarkable endurance and adherence to mitzvos. Lighting Shabbos candles links you in an unbroken chain back to our Matriarch Sarah and forms a bond destined to only be stronger into the future. Many have tried to break this holy link, but it has been the fortitude and the sacrifice of the Jewish women throughout the most challenging of times that ensures the Jewish candle burns as bright as ever.

To Search with a Candle

Shabbos is a day of searching and of penetrating exploration into who we are and what our life goals should be. It is a time where without the tension and ever-present distractions of the day-to-day routine we can focus on searching for that which has real meaning and value in life. It is a time where we can take stock of our true investments: our families, our relationships, ourselves, and our relationship with Hashem.

Candles are used to assist in the search for a lost item or to guide one in the darkness of the night. It is the light of the candle that sheds light, understanding, and clarity when things are dark and confusing. The *pasuk* says: נֵר ה׳ נִשְׁמַת אָדָם חֹפֵשׂ כָּל חַדְרֵי בָטֶן, *A man's soul is the lamp of Hashem, which **searches** the chambers of one's innards* (*Mishlei* 20:27).

The holy day of Shabbos is ushered in with candles as a means of urging us to use their light to seek that which is missing, for that which our souls are pining. Throughout the week we are busy, often becoming lost in the clamor of work, the media, shopping, and our daily responsibilities. When Shabbos arrives, it is time to find ourselves, search for our true priorities and meaning, find the light amid the dark, and forge a path in the dense forest. This is the message of the candles.

The Candle of Hashem Is the Soul of Man

It was Friday, *Parashas Vayakhel*, the 26th day of Adar 1935, at 2:30 p.m., just a few short hours before the onset of Shabbos, and Sara Schenirer, the famed founder of the Bais Yaakov school network, returned her soul to its Creator at the young age of 53. Word of the renowned teacher's passing spread rapidly as hundreds of her students began to stream to the Krakow Bais Yaakov Seminar, the original institution of the later illustrious Bais Yaakov school system.

Men, women, young and old, Rabbanim and Rebbes, bowed their heads in sorrow and mourning for the loss of the great Sara Schenirer who, nearly

single-handedly, against much opposition, transformed Jewish girls' education throughout the world. Her students eulogized her and hundreds of candles were lit in her memory. She was the *eim b'Yisrael* who, through her love, warmth, passion, intellect, and selflessness, sparked the flames of so many Jewish souls. She lovingly stoked the embers of so many and ensured that the lights of their souls would burn bright and proud.

That Erev Shabbos a great light of the Jewish people was extinguished. In its place, the hundreds and thousands of candles that Sara Schenirer kindled burned brightly. It is these candles that have continued to perpetuate her vision and continue to bless the Jewish nation with children and families that light up the world with their Torah and mitzvos. Although she never had any children of her own, no mother had as many children as she (see *Eim B'Yisrael,* Vol. 2, page 24; *Selected Writings of Rav Shimon Schwab,* page 324).

In the *tefillah* recited after candle lighting, women pray: וְהָאֵר נֵרֵנוּ שֶׁלֹּא יִכְבֶּה לְעוֹלָם וָעֶד, *and cause our light to illuminate that it not be extinguished forever.* Unlike a material candle that cannot remain lit forever, the *neshamah* of a Jew, which is compared to a candle, can burn bright and vibrant for eternity. How does one ensure that the *ner* of his soul burns for all eternity? Although a candle may be on its last portion of wax, flickering and nearly extinguished, it has the ability to kindle a new candle that will perpetuate the light of the first flame. We can light up the souls of others merely by paying them attention, giving them a smile, inquiring about their day, or lending a listening ear. We never know the effect of even the smallest of deeds, whether it be a word of encouragement, simple advice, or just going the extra step for those with whom we come in contact. There are countless stories of individuals who, through a simple deed, be it a smile, a small gift, a phone call, a letter, or even just a few dollars, have managed to transform the lives of others, thereby perpetuating the light of their own *neshamos.*

The Power of Candle Lighting

The home of the wife of the deceased prophet Ovadiah was bare; she was impoverished to the point where her creditors demanded her two children as slaves. She approached the prophet Elisha, begging him for help. Elisha asked her, "What can I do for you? Tell me, what have you in the house?" She replied, אֵין לְשִׁפְחָתְךָ כֹל בַּבַּיִת כִּי אִם אָסוּךְ שָׁמֶן, *"Your maidservant has nothing in the house except for a jar of oil"* (*Melachim II* 4:2).

Rabbi Yisroel Friedman, the Rebbe of Ruzhin, explains that Elisha asked the desperate woman in what merit should such a miracle be performed on her behalf: "Tell me, what do you have in the house? What merits and mitzvos have you done that can serve as a meritorious advocate on your behalf?" She then replied that women have three special mitzvos bestowed upon them: family purity, challah, and lighting Shabbos candles. The woman went on to explain that the mitzvah of family purity is not one that she can currently fulfill because she is a widow. She further noted that she does not have the ingredients in the home needed to bake bread, and therefore cannot perform the mitzvah of separating challah. The only mitzvah of the three special mitzvos women are charged with that she actively fulfills is kindling the Shabbos lights with the oil she has (אֵין לְשִׁפְחָתְךָ כֹל בַּבַּיִת כִּי אִם אָסוּךְ שָׁמֶן).

It was this mitzvah, the merit of candle lighting on the eve of Shabbos, which served as the catalyst for Elisha to have the ability to perform the miracle in which all the containers in her home filled with oil, supplying her with adequate funds to pay off her creditors and remain financially stable into the future. Such is the power of *neiros Shabbos*! (*Irin Kaddishin, Haftarah Parashas Va'eira*).

The Role of a Wife and Mother: Igniting the Spiritual Flames of Her Family

The Mishnah (*Shabbos* 2:7) says, "There are three things a man must say in his home on Erev Shabbos before dark: "*Esartem*, have you tithed? *Eravtem*, have you prepared the *eruv*? *Hadliku es haner*, kindle the Shabbos light!"

The *Chida* (*Pnei Dovid*) explains that "Erev Shabbos" is a reference to this world and "before dark" is a reference to the time before it is too late to make changes in this world. The man of the home tells his wife: *Esartem* — we have **already** amassed wealth (from the word *osher*, wealth). *Eravtem* — we have **already** attained sweetness and enjoyment from the pleasures of this world (from the word *areiv*, sweet*).* **Now, while we still have time,** *Hadliku es haner* — please kindle the fire of our souls, which are compared to a candle, as it says: נֵר ה׳ נִשְׁמַת אָדָם, *The candle of Hashem is the soul of man* (*Mishlei* 20:27). The mother and wife of the home has the capability and influence to ignite the souls of her family that pine and long for closeness to Hashem. It is her concern, encouragement, interest, and love that can spark the *neshamos* of her family.

The *Maharsha*, Rabbi Shmuel Eidels (*Sotah* 21a), explains that when Hashem told Moshe to teach the Jewish people about the Torah, He commanded: כֹּה תֹאמַר לְבֵית יַעֲקֹב וְתַגֵּיד לִבְנֵי יִשְׂרָאֵל, *So shall you say to the House of Yaakov and relate to the Children of Israel* (*Shemos* 19:3). *Rashi* comments that "the House of Yaakov" is referring to the Jewish women and "the Children of Israel" is referring to the Jewish men. Moshe was instructed to first teach the women Torah and mitzvos and only afterward to teach the men. This is because it is the women who have the persuasive power to influence the men and children to observe and adhere to the Torah and mitzvos! The women are the ones who can encourage and galvanize their husbands and children to learn Torah and observe mitzvos properly; they are the *Beis Yaakov,* the very foundation and energy of the Jewish home.

Here Lives a Jew!

Shabbos is most likely the single mitzvah that defines and identifies the Jewish people. One's level of observance is usually dictated by his Shabbos adherence. Likewise, Chazal tell us that one who guards the Shabbos is considered as if he kept the entire Torah, while one who desecrates the Shabbos is regarded as if he has violated the entire Torah. Shabbos is the heart of the Jewish body: It is the heart that nourishes every fiber of the human being (*Shem Olam*, Chapter 4).

> The Chafetz Chaim (Shem Olam, Chapter 1) explains this concept with a parable: A man requiring the services of a tailor walks to the tailor's place of business only to find the store closed. He looks around and notices that the tailor's sign is still prominently displayed and assumes that the tailor has just left for the day. The man returns a week later and notices the tailor's sign still prominently displayed, but the store is still closed. The man assumes that the tailor must have gone on vacation. A few days later he returns yet again and this time sees that the tailor's sign has been removed. He understands that the tailor's shop is no longer open for business.

Shabbos is called an אות, *sign*; it is the sign that clearly identifies one who safeguards its laws as a Jew. Even if a Jew has transgressed, he has not removed this sign exhibiting his Jewish identity. A

Jew is likened to the tailor who is not in his store but his sign remains prominently displayed. Shabbos is so essential and it defines our true identity.

When women usher in the Shabbos with the Friday-night candles they proclaim, "This home, my home, proudly carries the אוֹת, the distinguishing marker that asserts its Jewish identity. There may be bumps and difficulties along the way, but at the end of the day — כָּאן גָּר מִשְׁפַּחַת יְהוּדִי — here lives a Jewish family!"

We know that it is the Jewish women who determine the Jewishness of a child. If the mother is Jewish, then the child is Jewish. The Jewish women are the ones who merit gifting this אוֹת, this sign, that proclaims their children as being Jewish. Likewise, they are the ones to usher in the Shabbos that proudly identifies the inhabitants of the home as perpetuating the אוֹת of Shabbos that was given to us by Hashem.

The light of the Shabbos candles is what provides the electricity and the brightness to each Jewish home's אוֹת, the sign that so very much identifies and proclaims: כָּאן גָּר מִשְׁפַּחַת יְהוּדִי — here lives a Jewish family!

> *Two Jewish boys grew up together in the same neighborhood. One of these boys was raised in an observant home while the other was not. The non-religious boy was always envious of his religious counterpart, specifically when it came to the warm and inviting glow of the Shabbos neiros that his friend's mother would light each Friday before dark. He was drawn to the power of the neiros and asked his parents if they would start lighting Shabbos candles Friday night as well. They flatly refused. One Friday afternoon, the non-observant boy's parents went out for the evening and the boy was left alone in the house. He decided that if his parents did not want to light the Shabbos candles, then he would. The issue was that there was not a candle to be found in the house. After much searching, all that could be found were two yahrtzeit candles. Not knowing the difference, the young boy lit two yahrtzeit*

candles and was warmed by their glow. Eventually he fell asleep with a sense of pride that he had fulfilled this special mitzvah.

Hours later, the boy's parents returned and what they saw sent shivers up their spine. Two yahrtzeit candles, used to memorialize the deceased, whose meaning even they understood, stood on the table burning brightly. After a few moments, the man turned toward his wife and said, "Perhaps our son was correct after all. Maybe there was truth and meaning to his urging us to begin lighting Shabbos candles. Without the Shabbos candles and spirituality, perhaps we aren't really living, and memorial candles are truly appropriate for us" (Bishtei Einaim, page 311).

Candle Lighting — A Special Time for Prayer

It is well known that candle lighting is an exceptionally auspicious time for women's *tefillos*. *Rabbeinu Bachya* (*Shemos* 19:3) explains: It is the mother, who is generally in the home with her children, who through her power of love and emotion is the one to influence them to learn and live a life of Torah from the very youngest of ages. Because of this responsibility, it is meritorious for a woman to pray to Hashem at the time of candle lighting, a mitzvah imparted especially to her, that she merit children who light up the world with their Torah study. *Tefillos* are highly valued and accepted by Hashem at the time of a mitzvah performance. Thus, in the *zechus* of lighting Shabbos candles she should merit children filled with Torah which are, likewise, called a light, as the *pasuk* says (*Mishlei* 6:23): כִּי נֵר מִצְוָה וְתוֹרָה אוֹר, *For a commandment is a lamp and the Torah is light.* (See likewise *Rabbeinu Yonah, Iggeres HaTeshuvah* 81; *Mishnah Berurah* 263:3.)

It is the women's Shabbos candles that usher Shabbos into the home. Shabbos is the day of *emunah*, the time when all worries are stowed away and our relationship and reliance on Hashem is refreshed and fortified. The more a woman trusts in Hashem, the closer she is to Him, and the more propitious and dear her prayers are (see *Beis Elokim, Sha'ar HaTefillah*). It is therefore a special time for women to pray for themselves, their families, and for anything that they need, after kindling the Shabbos candles, a demonstration of *emunah* and a time of extreme closeness to Hashem.

Davening for Anything

At this special time for *tefillah* one must understand that there is nothing too small or trivial for which to reach out to Hashem. On the contrary, through *davening* to Hashem for even the smallest of issues or concerns, we fortify our belief that Hashem is involved in the most minute and mundane details of our life, and this is a source of blessing in and of itself. The Chazon Ish writes that one can *daven* to Hashem in any language he is comfortable with, and he should pray to Hashem "as one speaks to his friend" (*Kovetz Igros* 2:2; *Mesillas Yesharim* 19).

You can talk to Hashem on a moment-to-moment basis, in any language, without any formal preparations. All Hashem wants is our hearts. The *Sforno* (*Vayeitzei* 31:53) writes that the *tefillos* of a parent on behalf of her child are particularly effective. The mother of the great Rav Shmuel Kaidanover, a renowned Torah scholar and author, was a simple, unlearned woman who did not know how to read the Hebrew words of a siddur. Nevertheless, each Friday night by the Shabbos candles she would *daven* in her native Russian tongue, "Hashem, may it be Your will that my son Shmuel merit to be a *talmid chacham*." How those simple but pure *tefillos* were answered (see *Da'as Moshe, Parashas Terumah*).

We can ask Hashem for patience, good friendships, clarity, solace, the ability to accomplish, health, and anything that worries us or comes to mind. Rav Pinchos of Koritz, one of the foremost students of the Ba'al Shem Tov, was once overheard *davening* to Hashem with great concentration, "The helper should return." His students who had heard their Rebbi's *tefillah* were puzzled by its meaning and approached him about its nature. Rav Pinchos explained, "The cleaning lady that helps my wife at home left and my wife truly requires her help. I am therefore *davening* that the cleaning lady should return to work!" Rav Avraham from Slonim writes that when a child needs a new shirt or a quarter for the candy store he is not embarrassed to ask his father. The Jewish people are called *banim laMakom,* the children of Hashem, and therefore we can *daven* to Hashem for anything that we need, without hesitation, as each of us is a child of Hashem and He is our Father (*Bircas Avraham, Parashas Lech Lecha*).

A Time to Daven or …

The special moment has finally arrived. After a long and tiring week and a seemingly endless and exhausting day of preparations, the warm glow of Shabbos is finally here. The candles have just been lit and the mother of the home places her hands over her eyes, gathering her thoughts in preparation for using this special time, her time, to *daven* and talk to Hashem about her fears and worries, her needs and those of her family.

Just then, a piercing scream can be heard from upstairs, "Mommy, I can't find my Shabbos robe!" And then a little tug is felt from her three-year-old, "Mommy, I'm so hungry." Then the snowball effect really begins: "Mommy, Suri is annoying me." "Mommy, which shul did Tatty go to?" "Help, the lights are off in the bathroom." "Mommy, please,

I need help washing up," calls another from the bathroom. Mommy's frustration begins to mount, and if she has not already shouted for everyone to take hold of themselves for a few minutes, she thinks, *Can't I have five minutes, just five minutes to daven. Five minutes for me and Hashem at this special time?* What is intended to be a special, calm, connecting point to Hashem can within seconds morph into anger, frustration, and annoyance, the exact antithesis of the Shabbos spirit. What should a mother who may not have the time to *daven* at this special time think?

> One Rosh Hashanah, the townspeople of Berditchev waited anxiously for their Rebbe, Rav Levi Yitzchak, to begin blowing the shofar. Rav Levi Yitzchak, wrapped in his white tallis and kitel, walked up to the bimah with his shofar in hand and the congregation recited all the tefillos that precede shofar blowing. Yet, the Rebbe did not begin reciting the blessings and blow the shofar. Five minutes turned into nearly an hour delay.
>
> Rav Levi Yitzchak finally spoke, "Downstairs, at the entrance to the shul, sits a Jew who grew up in the house of a non-Jew and as such never received a Jewish education. The tefillos of the siddur are totally foreign to this simple man. He does not know how to read even the most basic tefillos. Yet, when he came to shul today and saw everyone davening with such intensity he was jealous and wanted to do the same. But what could he do? This simple Jew cried out to Hashem, 'Hashem, You know that I long to daven to You but I do not know how to read from the siddur. The only thing I recall is the Hebrew alphabet. I will therefore recite the aleph-beis, letter by letter, and please, Hashem, You combine the letters together to form a most beautiful and merciful tefillah.'
>
> "Over the last hour," said Rav Levi Yitzchak, "Hashem has been forming the most beautiful tefillos from the heartfelt aleph-beis prayer of this special Jew, and therefore we waited" (Yalkut Kedushas Levi, Rosh Hashanah, page 171).

When the children are begging for Mommy's attention know that you can condense your *davening*: "Hashem, You see that I want to stand here and pour my heart out to You. I want to tell You about my week, to thank You for the *berachah* You have bestowed upon me and my family and to pray for the future. But You have endowed me with other responsibilities, responsibilities that take precedence to this. Therefore, please take all the thoughts that You know are in my heart, and all the *tefillos* that You know I want to pour out to You, and all the *tefillos* for those I was going to *daven* for, and it should be as if I had prayed them to You in the most efficacious way." Undoubtedly, such a *tefillah* will have extraordinary and exceptional merits in the eyes of Hashem.

It is vital for a woman to understand that even if she has only 60 seconds to *daven* and then goes to tend to her children eager for her attention, the time spent with them *is actively accomplishing what her tefillos would*. What does this mean? In lieu of having the time to pray for her children's success and spiritual growth, a mother who lovingly gathers her children around her on the couch, hearing about their week, giving them attention, telling a story of *hashgachah pratis* that occurred to her that week, perhaps discussing the *parashah* or reading a book that strengthens their *emunah,* is actively transforming her children into what it is she would have *davened for* — secure, happy, and spiritually elevated children. When all is quiet and calm and a mother takes some time Friday night to bond with her children, hear their hearts, or tell them inspirational stories, she is an active participant in building her children into what she *davens* for: חֲכָמִים וּנְבוֹנִים, אוֹהֲבֵי ה', יִרְאֵי אֱלֹקִים, אַנְשֵׁי אֱמֶת, זֶרַע קֹדֶשׁ, בַּה' דְּבֵקִים, וּמְאִירִים אֶת הָעוֹלָם בַּתּוֹרָה וּבְמַעֲשִׂים טוֹבִים, וּבְכָל מְלֶאכֶת עֲבוֹדַת הַבּוֹרֵא, *wise and understanding, who love Hashem and fear God, people of truth, holy offspring, attached to Hashem, who illuminate the world with Torah and good deeds and with every labor in the service of the Creator.*

Davening for Others

Candle lighting is a special time to *daven* for those in need. We are all aware of a family member, friend, or neighbor who is looking for a *shidduch*, needs financial assistance, is challenged with an illness, struggling to have children or raise the ones they have, and the list goes on. Although at times we may not have the financial or physical ability to help those in need around us, we can always remember their plight in our *tefillos*, which may be the true source of strength they need. The Talmud (*Bava Kamma* 92a) states the unbelievable strength and efficaciousness of a prayer emanating from one who *davens* for another at a time when he is experiencing the identical hardship. Just recently the growing Jewish community of Cincinnati began an "I will *daven* for you and you *daven* for me" initiative as a merit for the community's fifteen girls looking for *shidduchim*. In miraculous fashion, each of these girls has since found her *shidduch* a mere short while after the program was initiated.

Rabbi Boruch Mordechai Ezrachi shares the following amazing story about a couple who were childless for many years. After long painful years of treatments and *tefillos* the husband decided to ask a well-known Rebbe for a blessing. The man told the Rebbe about all that he and his wife had gone through and if he could please bless them with a child. The Rebbe told him with pain on his face that he too has a son who is childless for many years. The Rebbe thought for a moment and said, "The Talmud (ibid.) states that one who *davens* for his friend and he needs that same thing will be answered first. Therefore, I suggest that we call my son, and upon your mutual agreements you will begin *davening* for him and he will begin *davening* for you." Both the husband and the Rebbe's son wholeheartedly agreed to the "deal," placing their *emunah* in the Talmud's promise of one who *davens* on behalf of another with a similar predicament. From that day forward both husbands *davened* with tremendous concentration that the other should merit children. Within that year each of the couples was blessed with a baby, and the babies were born on the *very same day*! (*Ish L'Rei'eihu, Parashas Lech Lecha,* page 96).

Thank You, Hashem, for a Beautiful Week

Imagine you had brought a cake or challah to a new neighbor and they never called to thank you. Imagine you had sent a gift to a teacher and they never sent home a note, called you, or mentioned the gift and their appreciation at that night's parent-teacher conference. Although we are required to judge these people and their lack of appreciation favorably, it takes a *gibor,* one who is strong in his *emunah,* to positively extend himself to those individuals once again. But imagine that the new neighbor walks over Shabbos afternoon or calls you after Shabbos, thanking you warmly for the delicious challah and saying how significant your gesture of friendship was. Imagine your child's teacher sending you a short note as to how meaningful your gift was and how your child adds such joy to the class. Ostensibly, in all these cases, the recipient's appreciation is itself a vehicle that drives and influences you to want to give again and more in the future. Such is the power of *hakaras hatov,* appreciation. The same holds true with our demonstration of appreciation for all that Hashem does for us; it is not only proper but is a fountain of additional *berachah* from Hashem as well (see *Rabbeinu Bachya, Bereishis* 32:11).

The precious minutes after candle lighting can be used not only to beseech Hashem for all our needs but to look back and see the wonderful good Hashem has bestowed upon us over the past week. The *pasuk* says (*Tehillim* 105:3): יִשְׂמַח לֵב מְבַקְשֵׁי ה׳, *glad will be the heart of those who seek Hashem.* Rav Yechezkel

Abramsky defines the *mevakshei Hashem* as those who seek and search for Hashem's guiding Hand in all of their daily experiences and in every event. It is these people who merit true happiness (*Melech B'Yofyav,* page 609; see also *Yesodos HaChinuch,* Rav Hirsch, in a letter to women, page 142).

Take a few minutes to recall how you saw the Hand of Hashem (*hashgachah pratis*) in your life over this past week. Was it a friend that you met, a job opportunity that came from an unexpected source, an item you wanted that unexpectedly went on sale, a good report from the teacher, an inspirational message at a time of need, and the list goes on. Even for something small and seemingly trivial, seek Hashem in your life and thank Him. The Shabbos table is an exceptional time to share your personal incidents of *hashgachah pratis* with your family. Likewise, involve your children or even guests to bring to light how they have seen Hashem's involvement in their lives over the past week. This is a wonderful and engaging means of bringing *emunah* in Hashem's ever-guiding Presence alive and personal.

The Power of Tefillos to Kindle the Soul

Ten-year-old Moshe experienced great difficulty in yeshivah. Although he tried very hard to pay attention and follow the lessons, nothing clicked. While all his friends participated and enjoyed class, Moshe sat there distraught over his inability to learn Torah and understand his rebbi. Moshe's parents were totally dedicated to helping him and took him to a number of learning disability specialists, all the while enlisting the services of private tutors, but to no avail. The pain of Moshe and his parents was agonizing.

At one point in the middle of the school year, Moshe's rebbi noticed some positive changes. At first Moshe was more attentive, as if he were following the lesson. Then a few days later Moshe began participating in class until eventually he was asking inquisitive questions. Moshe's rebbi phoned his parents, wanting to give them the joyous report about their son's amazing improvement. The rebbi was also curious to know how such a turnaround had occurred.

Upon hearing the rebbi's wonderful report, Moshe's mother recounted what had happened. "Over the last few months, Moshe has been coming home crying, pouring out his heart to me over his desire to learn Torah and understand what was being taught. 'How long can I go on like this?' Moshe would cry to me. His tears pained my heart. I told Moshe that when a mother lights candles on the eve of Shabbos it is an extremely auspicious time for her to daven that her children succeed in their Torah study. I always daven for your success but now I am going to daven with even greater concentration and intensity. I want you to come and stand next to me while I light the Shabbos candles, and you and I will daven together. Hopefully both of our tefillos and cries will be accepted by Hashem.

"That very Erev Shabbos, Moshe stood next to me as I lit the Shabbos candles. We then began to daven together and I heard Moshe, my little 10-year-old tzaddik, cry out to Hashem that he should have success in his learning. Moshe's tefillos and tears mingled with mine in a harmonious plea to Hashem. This has been going on for the last few weeks and baruch Hashem our tefillos are being answered" (Barchi Nafshi, Vol. 4, page 352).

A Warm Tear

Rabbi Moshe Sherer, the visionary leader of the Agudath Israel of America, believed that it was his mother's tefillos and tears that served as the catalyst for all his myriad achievements and absolute

dedication to a life of furthering the needs of the Jewish people. Especially memorable was Mrs. Sherer's Shabbos candle lighting, a time in which she would pour out her heart in great concentration. As a young child, Moshe was curious to know what his mother davened for by the neiros and one time he hid under the table. What he heard greatly impacted the direction he chose to take in life. Three times, with immense concentration and feeling, Mrs. Sherer davened, "Ribbono Shel Olam, baleichten zolst Du di oigen fun meina kinderlach in Dein heilige Torah — Please, Hashem, light up my children's eyes through the precious words of Your holy Torah."

Despite it being the height of the Depression and the Sherer home lacking so many basic staples, what was most important to Mrs. Sherer was that her children lead a life of Torah. At that special moment, a warm tear fell from his mother's eyes into young Moshe's open palm sticking out from under the table. It was a tear of הַזֹּרְעִים בְּדִמְעָה בְּרִנָּה יִקְצֹרוּ, those who tearfully sow will reap in glad song (Tehillim 126:5). It was a tear that never dried from the hand of Rabbi Sherer, always encouraging, guiding, and spurring him on to greater accomplishments. It was his mother's focus on priorities to which Rabbi Sherer attributed his own dedicated and selfless service of the Jewish people and the great success of the Agudath Israel of America (Rabbi Sherer, ArtScroll/Mesorah, page 44; as told to the author by Rabbi Shimshon Sherer).

The Everlasting Light of the Shabbos Candles

Although a candle does not remain lit indefinitely, its light has the ability to steer one in the right direction, leading to an everlasting change.

Even a short burst of light can provide enough illumination and clarity so as to locate the correct door or a lost object. The Shabbos candles do not just light up the home for the few hours they are lit, but rather have the potential to illuminate the heart and soul of children and families for generations to come. The *tefillos* that a mother pours out for her husband and children give them strength, fortitude, and Heavenly assistance to face any challenges that life may bring and bring them merit to be beacons of light for the Jewish nation.

Through merely gazing upon students in the yeshivah, the Chazon Ish could distinguish how one student's mother had cried while lighting the Shabbos candles that her child should grow up to be a Torah scholar while the other student's mother did not cry. Such is the power of a mother's *tefillos* at this auspicious time. The Chazon Ish would likewise comment that even a child who was not blessed with exceptional intelligence but nevertheless puts all his efforts into his learning and prospers is successful because of his mother's or grandmother's *tefillos* and tears shed at candle lighting (*M'Be'er HaShabbos,* page 76; *Hi Tis'halel,* page 237). A young Rabbi Moshe Sternbuch once recited a novel Torah thought to the great Tchebiner Rav, Rabbi Dov Berish Weidenfeld. The Tchebiner Rav looked at the young Moshe and said, "What you said now was not your original thought. Rather, it was your mother's. It was in the merit of your mother's *tefillos* at candle lighting that you are capable of constructing such a beautiful and novel Torah thought."

Someone once approached the Brisker Rav for a blessing that his son merit to be a Torah scholar and a God-fearing Jew. The Brisker Rav responded, "Why do you seek my blessings? If it is truly your will that your son be a *talmid chacham,* then you yourself must go and learn Torah as well as learn with your son. If it is your will that your son be a God-fearing Jew then take my advice, have your wife pour out her heart at candle lighting that your child should merit fear of Heaven" (ibid. page 77).

A woman standing in front of the candles praying for herself and her family needs to know that each and every one of her *tefillos* is precious in the eyes of Hashem, Who is ever attentively listening. Although at times unnoticeable, every single *tefillah* without exception is heard and accepted by Hashem, Who ensures its merits are used when needed most.

The Memory of a Mother's Shabbos Candle Tefillos

Regarding the *ben sorer u'moreh*, the wayward son who is punished with death, the *pasuk* (*Devarim* 21:18) says that the child did not listen to the voice of his father and the voice of his mother and that was the ultimate reason for his spiritual downfall and subsequent punishment. The Kotzker Rebbe explains that the reason the child fell to such depths is because *he did not hear the voice of his father* — singing the words of Torah; and *he did not hear the voice of his mother* — pouring out her heart to Hashem at candle lighting or praying at other times. Children naturally have a deep attachment to their parents and seek to follow in their ways. The *tefillos* and the sight of a mother *davening* by her *neiros* remains imprinted on children's memories forever, continuously providing them with strength and the desire to likewise turn to Hashem and pour out their hearts in *tefillah*.

A well-known individual with a beautiful family living in Brooklyn shared the following story about himself:

> *A teenager in his early teens who had come from a rabbinic home had survived the terror of the Nazi death camps, but his soul had been all but extinguished. This young man remained in the Displaced Persons camps, incapable of putting on tefillin or keeping Shabbos. One day Rabbi*

Yekusiel Yehudah Halberstam, the Klausenberger Rebbe, who himself had suffered indescribable torture and had lost his wife and eleven children, spotted this young man. The Rebbe befriended him and took him under his wing. The Rebbe did not demand that the young man put on tefillin, keep Shabbos, or come to shul.

The young man recounted, "The Rebbe took care of me and I would drift in and out of his beis midrash without keeping mitzvos. Yet the Rebbe's powerful and awe-inspiring tefillos shook me to the core and I felt the need to talk to the Rebbe and bare my soul. Little did I know that the Rebbe also wanted to talk to me.

"After his Thursday-night shiur on the parashah the Rebbe motioned me over and we began to walk. The Rebbe asked me how I was, if I was forming any friendships with the other boys in the camp, and so on. The Rebbe turned to me and asked, 'Do you remember your parents' home from before the war?' I nodded my head in affirmation, longingly recalling a vanished era. The Rebbe continued, 'Do you recall the faces of your father and mother?' Again, I nodded my head affirmatively. The Rebbe continued to ask me, 'Do you remember your mother, may she rest in peace, when she kindled the Shabbos candles on Erev Shabbos as tears streamed down her face? Do you not know what she was crying for and what she was davening to Hashem for? I will tell you, she was praying that she merit ehrliche kinderlach and that her children go in the path of Hashem. Now that she has left this world and sanctified Hashem's Name, should her desire cease? Have her tefillos and tears gone to waste? Who will see that your mother's tefillos are fulfilled if not you?'

"The Rebbe's piercing words that emanated directly from his heart struck me like a bolt of lightning and I began to cry uncontrollably. I realized that I, as the only surviving member of our family, was responsible to ensure that the tefillos of my dear mother for righteous children and

grandchildren would be fulfilled. The tears flowed incessantly. It was after an hour of tears that I began to calm down a bit. The Rebbe said to me, 'Stay with us, come to our beis midrash and it will be good for you. Anything you need I will take care of. Ask me for anything you may need like a child requests of his father.' I remained with the Rebbe … for life" (Lapid Ha'Eish, Vol. 1, page 346).

The Power of a Mother's Tefillos at Candle Lighting

The Heiman family from Israel is a beautiful family with renowned superlative character traits and dedication to Torah and mitzvos. One of the family members divulged a family secret as to their success.

> My grandmother was not religious. But, she always lit candles Friday night before sundown and prayed for the success of her children and grandchildren, remembering that her mother had likewise done so back in Europe. What kind of success did she have in mind when she prayed for her family? Well, her husband, my grandfather, worked for then-Prime Minister David Ben-Gurion and would come home every day praising his boss's talents, skills, and brilliance. Impressed by these accolades, my grandmother would pray every Friday night after lighting candles that her children and grandchildren should grow up to be like Prime Minister Ben-Gurion.
>
> One day, the prime minister met with Rav Avrohom Yeshaya Karelitz, the famed Chazon Ish, in a well-publicized meeting. After the meeting, Prime Minister Ben-Gurion called all of his staff together, including my grandfather, lauding the venerable sage's unmatched penetrating brilliance and deep perception in all subject matters.
>
> My grandfather came home that day, and as

usual reported the highlights of what the prime minister had said at the office. Upon hearing Ben-Gurion's praise for the Chazon Ish and how he had never met such a giant of a man, my grandmother reasoned that if the prime minister held the Chazon Ish in such high regard, she would start praying after Shabbos candle lighting that her children and grandchildren merit to be like the Chazon Ish, and not like the prime minister!

It appears that the awesome power of a woman's tefillos at the time of candle lighting made all the difference for our family! *(L'Ha'eir, page 20; Tiv HaNissuin, page 288).*

Lighting Up the World

A child of a well-known non-observant Israeli personality was *chozer b'teshuvah* and became an outstanding Torah scholar. When asked what merit initiated this man's return to Judaism, the Chazon Ish responded, "It was because of a grandmother or a great-grandmother from generations gone by who would stand by the Shabbos candles praying that her offspring merit to be righteous, God-fearing Jews. Even one *tefillah*, even one tear is never lost. It was in this merit, generations later, that her progeny returned to a Torah way of life" *(Ma'aseh Ish,* Vol. 7, page 24; see likewise *Chayei Olam,* Chapter 28).

> *The difficult but necessary decision was made. The dean and rebbeim of the yeshivah decided that a specific student was having a negative influence on the other students and he was asked to leave. The severity of the situation had been unknown to the student's mother, who came crying to the dean with the following words, "Rosh Yeshivah, why did you not tell me earlier what was transpiring? Had I known the severity of my son's situation I would have davened with great*

concentration and fervor and things may have not spiraled down to this point!" Upon hearing the pure words of this mother, the Rosh Yeshivah said, "You are correct, your tefillos for your child are indeed ever-powerful and we did not afford you the opportunity to pray. Therefore, we will allow your son to come back to the school" (Darchei HaChaim, page 22).

The Tears of a Mother Melt the Hardest of Hearts

The sight of a mother crying for the success of her children is a sight that can pierce even the strongest and most hardened souls.

Rabbi Gamliel Rabinowitz, the famed Yerushalmi Rav, recounts the following story in which he was directly involved:

"One day I received a frantic call from a woman calling from the United States. She had a teenage son with whom I had had some connection years back. Subsequently, years later he had forsaken his religious upbringing. The mother was at a total loss as to what to do with her son. Although she loved him dearly, she was deeply pained by his deviant behavior and confrontationist nature that had thrown their home into an abyss of agony and anguish. The mother was unaware of the correct path to take. Should their child be told to leave the home, or should they allow him to remain home and continue to provide him their love despite his absolute disrespect, defiance, and total disregard of his parents?

"After weighing the various options and of having firsthand knowledge regarding the family, I instructed the mother to allow the child to remain at home. As long as the child continues to come home each day it is a sign that he still values and

clings to his parents and the warm atmosphere of the home. It would be criminal to damage that link, especially considering that there were no other children at home. The mother began to cry, 'But what should we do? The situation cannot continue as is! We are breaking!' After much thought I suggested as follows: The Talmud (Yevamos 65b) tells us that just like there is a time and place to say something, there is a time and place to say nothing. In this instance, where each conversation about your son's behavior erupts into a massive fight and power struggle, I believe it would be better for you not to say anything. Do not comment on his behavior, do not enter into any confrontations with him. But I will tell you what to do. Accept upon yourself Shabbos 30 minutes early. After candle lighting, which as you know is a tremendous eis ratzon, a propitious time for prayer, daven to Hashem that He should have mercy on the neshamah of your child and his soul should merit to be pure like the day he was born."

The next week, this mother lit her Shabbos candles 30 minutes early as per Rabbi Gamliel's instructions and began davening for her child. Immediately, torrents of tears burst forth from her eyes and the cries of her pained heart could be heard throughout the home.

After some time, her tears let up and she began to set the Shabbos table. Her son, who was upstairs in his room, had heard his mother's weeping and approached her with much concern. "Mommy, are you okay? Why were you crying so much by hadlakas neiros?" The mother replied that she was fine. Yet, the powerful tears of his mother penetrated deeply into the heart of the troubled teenager, even though outwardly there was no apparent change. A pattern began to develop. The boy and his parents no longer argued and debated about his behavior. His mother washed his laundry and cooked for him, and he was happy that he could continue his own lifestyle while still having his physical needs met.

Yet, every Erev Shabbos his mother would light candles early and then break into heartrending tears, davening to Hashem with tremendous concentration and emotion for the plight of her son.

A few weeks passed and I received a call from an ebullient mother. The sight of the mother week in and week out crying in front of the Shabbos candles, pleading with Hashem that her son return to the ways of Hashem, had stirred something deep inside the boy's soul. He was changing. He had begun to keep Shabbos, learn Torah, and return to his pure roots. The profound effect of a mother's tears, a mother so intertwined with her child, had the profound ability to melt the hardest of hearts and rekindle the embers of her precious son's soul (Tiv HaNissuin, page 244).

The Birth of Shmuel Hanavi and Tefillas Chanah

The *Shelah HaKadosh* (*Shabbos, Ner Mitzvah* 26) writes that at candle lighting, it is meritorious for women to recite the *Haftarah* for the first day of Rosh Hashanah, which recounts the story of Chanah, her painful barrenness, her subsequent *tefillos* for her son Shmuel, and her song of prayer. Some explain that reading these passages is meritorious for women who have not as of yet had children or women who are having difficulty raising their children. These passages are found in *Shmuel I* 1:1–2:10 (*Kitzur Shulchan Aruch* 75:2).

וַיְהִי אִישׁ אֶחָד מִן הָרָמָתַיִם צוֹפִים מֵהַר אֶפְרָיִם וּשְׁמוֹ אֶלְקָנָה בֶּן יְרֹחָם בֶּן אֱלִיהוּא בֶּן תֹּחוּ בֶן צוּף אֶפְרָתִי. וְלוֹ שְׁתֵּי נָשִׁים שֵׁם אַחַת חַנָּה וְשֵׁם הַשֵּׁנִית פְּנִנָּה וַיְהִי לִפְנִנָּה יְלָדִים וּלְחַנָּה אֵין יְלָדִים. וְעָלָה הָאִישׁ הַהוּא מֵעִירוֹ מִיָּמִים יָמִימָה לְהִשְׁתַּחֲוֺת וְלִזְבֹּחַ לַיהוה צְבָאוֹת בְּשִׁלֹה וְשָׁם שְׁנֵי בְנֵי עֵלִי חָפְנִי וּפִנְחָס כֹּהֲנִים לַיהוה. וַיְהִי הַיּוֹם וַיִּזְבַּח אֶלְקָנָה וְנָתַן לִפְנִנָּה אִשְׁתּוֹ וּלְכָל בָּנֶיהָ וּבְנוֹתֶיהָ מָנוֹת. וּלְחַנָּה יִתֵּן מָנָה אַחַת אַפָּיִם כִּי אֶת

חַנָּה אָהֵב וַיהוה סָגַר רַחְמָהּ. וְכִעֲסַתָּה צָרָתָהּ גַּם כַּעַס בַּעֲבוּר הַרְעִמָהּ כִּי סָגַר יהוה בְּעַד רַחְמָהּ. וְכֵן יַעֲשֶׂה שָׁנָה בְשָׁנָה מִדֵּי עֲלֹתָהּ בְּבֵית יהוה כֵּן תַּכְעִסֶנָּה וַתִּבְכֶּה וְלֹא תֹאכַל. וַיֹּאמֶר לָהּ אֶלְקָנָה אִישָׁהּ חַנָּה לָמֶה תִבְכִּי וְלָמֶה לֹא תֹאכְלִי וְלָמֶה יֵרַע לְבָבֵךְ הֲלוֹא אָנֹכִי טוֹב לָךְ מֵעֲשָׂרָה בָּנִים. וַתָּקָם חַנָּה אַחֲרֵי אָכְלָה בְשִׁלֹה וְאַחֲרֵי שָׁתֹה וְעֵלִי הַכֹּהֵן יֹשֵׁב עַל הַכִּסֵּא עַל מְזוּזַת הֵיכַל יהוה. וְהִיא מָרַת נָפֶשׁ וַתִּתְפַּלֵּל עַל יהוה וּבָכֹה תִבְכֶּה. וַתִּדֹּר נֶדֶר וַתֹּאמַר יהוה צְבָאוֹת אִם רָאֹה תִרְאֶה בָּעֳנִי אֲמָתֶךָ וּזְכַרְתַּנִי וְלֹא תִשְׁכַּח אֶת אֲמָתֶךָ וְנָתַתָּה לַאֲמָתְךָ זֶרַע אֲנָשִׁים וּנְתַתִּיו לַיהוה כָּל יְמֵי חַיָּיו וּמוֹרָה לֹא יַעֲלֶה עַל רֹאשׁוֹ. וְהָיָה כִּי הִרְבְּתָה לְהִתְפַּלֵּל לִפְנֵי יהוה וְעֵלִי שֹׁמֵר אֶת פִּיהָ. וְחַנָּה הִיא מְדַבֶּרֶת עַל לִבָּהּ רַק שְׂפָתֶיהָ נָּעוֹת וְקוֹלָהּ לֹא יִשָּׁמֵעַ וַיַּחְשְׁבֶהָ עֵלִי לְשִׁכֹּרָה. וַיֹּאמֶר אֵלֶיהָ עֵלִי עַד מָתַי תִּשְׁתַּכָּרִין הָסִירִי אֶת יֵינֵךְ מֵעָלָיִךְ. וַתַּעַן חַנָּה וַתֹּאמֶר לֹא אֲדֹנִי אִשָּׁה קְשַׁת רוּחַ אָנֹכִי וְיַיִן וְשֵׁכָר לֹא שָׁתִיתִי וָאֶשְׁפֹּךְ אֶת נַפְשִׁי לִפְנֵי יהוה. אַל תִּתֵּן אֶת אֲמָתְךָ לִפְנֵי בַּת בְּלִיָּעַל כִּי מֵרֹב שִׂיחִי וְכַעְסִי דִּבַּרְתִּי עַד הֵנָּה. וַיַּעַן עֵלִי וַיֹּאמֶר לְכִי לְשָׁלוֹם וֵאלֹהֵי יִשְׂרָאֵל יִתֵּן אֶת שֵׁלָתֵךְ אֲשֶׁר שָׁאַלְתְּ מֵעִמּוֹ. וַתֹּאמֶר תִּמְצָא שִׁפְחָתְךָ חֵן בְּעֵינֶיךָ וַתֵּלֶךְ הָאִשָּׁה לְדַרְכָּהּ וַתֹּאכַל וּפָנֶיהָ לֹא הָיוּ לָהּ עוֹד. וַיַּשְׁכִּמוּ בַבֹּקֶר וַיִּשְׁתַּחֲווּ לִפְנֵי יהוה וַיָּשֻׁבוּ וַיָּבֹאוּ אֶל בֵּיתָם הָרָמָתָה וַיֵּדַע אֶלְקָנָה אֶת חַנָּה אִשְׁתּוֹ וַיִּזְכְּרֶהָ יהוה. וַיְהִי לִתְקֻפוֹת הַיָּמִים וַתַּהַר חַנָּה וַתֵּלֶד בֵּן וַתִּקְרָא אֶת שְׁמוֹ שְׁמוּאֵל כִּי מֵיהוה שְׁאִלְתִּיו. וַיַּעַל הָאִישׁ אֶלְקָנָה וְכָל בֵּיתוֹ לִזְבֹּחַ לַיהוה אֶת זֶבַח הַיָּמִים וְאֶת נִדְרוֹ. וְחַנָּה לֹא עָלָתָה כִּי אָמְרָה לְאִישָׁהּ עַד יִגָּמֵל הַנַּעַר וַהֲבִאֹתִיו וְנִרְאָה אֶת פְּנֵי יהוה וְיָשַׁב שָׁם עַד עוֹלָם. וַיֹּאמֶר לָהּ אֶלְקָנָה אִישָׁהּ עֲשִׂי הַטּוֹב בְּעֵינַיִךְ שְׁבִי עַד גָּמְלֵךְ אֹתוֹ

אַךְ יָקֵם יהוה אֶת דְּבָרוֹ וַתֵּשֶׁב הָאִשָּׁה וַתֵּינֶק אֶת בְּנָהּ עַד גָּמְלָהּ אֹתוֹ. וַתַּעֲלֵהוּ עִמָּהּ כַּאֲשֶׁר גְּמָלַתּוּ בְּפָרִים שְׁלֹשָׁה וְאֵיפָה אַחַת קֶמַח וְנֵבֶל יַיִן וַתְּבִאֵהוּ בֵית יהוה שִׁלוֹ וְהַנַּעַר נָעַר. וַיִּשְׁחֲטוּ אֶת הַפָּר וַיָּבִיאוּ אֶת הַנַּעַר אֶל עֵלִי. וַתֹּאמֶר בִּי אֲדֹנִי חֵי נַפְשְׁךָ אֲדֹנִי אֲנִי הָאִשָּׁה הַנִּצֶּבֶת עִמְּכָה בָּזֶה לְהִתְפַּלֵּל אֶל יהוה. אֶל הַנַּעַר הַזֶּה הִתְפַּלָּלְתִּי וַיִּתֵּן יהוה לִי אֶת שְׁאֵלָתִי אֲשֶׁר שָׁאַלְתִּי מֵעִמּוֹ. וְגַם אָנֹכִי הִשְׁאִלְתִּהוּ לַיהוה כָּל הַיָּמִים אֲשֶׁר הָיָה הוּא שָׁאוּל לַיהוה וַיִּשְׁתַּחוּ שָׁם לַיהוה. וַתִּתְפַּלֵּל חַנָּה וַתֹּאמַר עָלַץ לִבִּי בַּיהוה רָמָה קַרְנִי בַּיהוה רָחַב פִּי עַל אוֹיְבַי כִּי שָׂמַחְתִּי בִּישׁוּעָתֶךָ. אֵין קָדוֹשׁ כַּיהוה כִּי אֵין בִּלְתֶּךָ וְאֵין צוּר כֵּאלֹהֵינוּ. אַל תַּרְבּוּ תְדַבְּרוּ גְּבֹהָה גְבֹהָה יֵצֵא עָתָק מִפִּיכֶם כִּי אֵל דֵּעוֹת יהוה וְלוֹ נִתְכְּנוּ עֲלִלוֹת. קֶשֶׁת גִּבֹּרִים חַתִּים וְנִכְשָׁלִים אָזְרוּ חָיִל. שְׂבֵעִים בַּלֶּחֶם נִשְׂכָּרוּ וּרְעֵבִים חָדֵלּוּ עַד עֲקָרָה יָלְדָה שִׁבְעָה וְרַבַּת בָּנִים אֻמְלָלָה. יהוה מֵמִית וּמְחַיֶּה מוֹרִיד שְׁאוֹל וַיָּעַל. יהוה מוֹרִישׁ וּמַעֲשִׁיר מַשְׁפִּיל אַף מְרוֹמֵם. מֵקִים מֵעָפָר דָּל מֵאַשְׁפֹּת יָרִים אֶבְיוֹן לְהוֹשִׁיב עִם נְדִיבִים וְכִסֵּא כָבוֹד יַנְחִלֵם כִּי לַיהוה מְצֻקֵי אֶרֶץ וַיָּשֶׁת עֲלֵיהֶם תֵּבֵל. רַגְלֵי חֲסִידָיו יִשְׁמֹר וּרְשָׁעִים בַּחֹשֶׁךְ יִדָּמּוּ כִּי לֹא בְכֹחַ יִגְבַּר אִישׁ. יהוה יֵחַתּוּ מְרִיבָיו עָלָיו בַּשָּׁמַיִם יַרְעֵם יהוה יָדִין אַפְסֵי אָרֶץ וְיִתֶּן עֹז לְמַלְכּוֹ וְיָרֵם קֶרֶן מְשִׁיחוֹ.

There was a certain man from Ramathaim-zophim, from Mount Ephraim, whose name was Elkanah, son of Jeroham, son of Elihu, son of Tohu, son of Zuph, from the land of Ephraim. He had two wives; one's name was Hannah and the second's name was Peninnah. Peninnah had children, but Hannah had no children. This man would ascend from his city from year to year to prostrate himself and to bring offerings to HASHEM, Master of Legions, in Shiloh, where the two sons of Eli — Hophni and

Phinehas — were Kohanim to HASHEM. It happened on the day that Elkanah brought offerings that he gave portions to Peninnah, his wife, and to all her sons and daughters. But to Hannah he gave a double portion, for he loved Hannah and HASHEM had closed her womb. Her rival [Peninnah] provoked her again and again in order to irritate her, for HASHEM had closed her womb. This is what he would do year after year, and whenever [Peninnah] would go up to the house of HASHEM, she would provoke her; she would cry and not eat. Elkanah, her husband, said to her, "Hannah, why do you cry and why do you not eat? Why is your heart broken? Am I not better to you than ten children?" Hannah arose after eating in Shiloh and after drinking; and Eli the Kohen was sitting on the chair, near the doorpost of the Sanctuary of HASHEM. She was feeling bitter, and she prayed to HASHEM, weeping continuously. She made a vow and said, "HASHEM, Master of Legions, if You take note of the suffering of Your maidservant, and You remember me, and do not forget Your maidservant, and give Your maidservant male offspring, then I shall give him to HASHEM all the days of his life, and a razor shall not come upon his head." It happened as she continued to pray before HASHEM that Eli observed her mouth. Hannah was speaking to her heart — only her lips moved, but her voice was not heard — so Eli thought she was drunk. Eli said to her, "How long will you be drunk? Remove your wine from yourself!" Hannah answered and said, "No, my lord, I am a woman of aggrieved spirit. I have drunk neither wine nor strong drink, and I have poured out my soul before HASHEM. Do not deem your maidservant to be a base woman — for it is out of much grievance and anger that I have spoken until now." Eli then answered and said, "Go in peace. The God of Israel will grant the request you have made of Him." She said, "May your maidservant find favor in your eyes." Then the woman went on her way and she ate, and no longer had the same look on her face. They arose early in the morning and prostrated

themselves before HASHEM; then they returned and came to their home, to Ramah. Elkanah knew Hannah his wife and HASHEM remembered her. And it happened with the passage of the period of days that Hannah had conceived, and she gave birth to a son. She named him Samuel, for [she said,] "I requested him from HASHEM." The man Elkanah ascended with his entire household to bring to HASHEM the annual offering and his vow. But Hannah did not ascend, as she told her husband, "When the child is weaned, then I will bring him, and he shall appear before HASHEM and shall settle there forever." Elkanah her husband said to her, "Do what is good in your eyes; remain until you wean him — but may HASHEM fulfill His word." So the woman remained and nursed her son until she weaned him. She brought him up with her when she weaned him, with three bulls, one ephah of flour, and a flask of wine; she brought him to the house of HASHEM in Shiloh, though the child was still tender. They slaughtered the bull, and brought the child to Eli. She said, "Please, my lord! By your life, my lord, I am the woman who was standing by you here praying to HASHEM. This is the child that I prayed for; HASHEM granted me my request that I asked of Him. Furthermore, I have dedicated him to HASHEM — all the days that he lives he is dedicated to HASHEM." He then prostrated himself to HASHEM. Then Hannah prayed and said: My heart exults in HASHEM, my pride has been raised through HASHEM; my mouth is opened wide against my antagonists, for I rejoice in Your salvation. There is none as holy as HASHEM, for there is none besides You, and there is no Rock like our God. Do not abound in speaking with arrogance upon arrogance, let not haughtiness come from your mouth; for HASHEM is the God of thoughts, and [men's] deeds are accounted by Him The bow of the mighty is broken, while the foundering are girded with strength. The sated ones are hired out for bread, while the hungry ones cease to be so; while the barren woman bears seven, the one with many children becomes bereft. HASHEM brings death and gives life, He lowers to the grave and raises up. HASHEM impoverishes and makes rich, He humbles and He elevates. He raises the needy from the dirt, from the trash heaps He lifts the destitute, to seat [them] with nobles and to endow them with a seat of honor — for HASHEM's are the pillars of the earth, and upon them He set the world. He guards the steps of His devout ones, but the wicked are stilled in darkness; for not through strength does man prevail. HASHEM — may those who contend with Him be shattered, let the heavens thunder against them. May HASHEM judge to the ends of the earth; may He give power to His king and raise the pride of His anointed one.

Yom Tov Candle Lighting

When to Light:

On the first of two Yom Tov nights:

❖ When both Erev Yom Tov and the first of the two days of Yom Tov occur during the week, there are different customs regarding when to light the candles. Rav Yosef Falk, in his introduction to the *sefer Drisha* authored by his father, Rabbi Yehoshua Falk, lauds his mother Baila for her magnanimous spirit and noble deeds. He writes that his mother opined that women should light the Yom Tov candles *prior* to the start of Yom Tov just as Shabbos candles are lit before the start of Shabbos. Some follow this opinion, while others have the custom to wait until the men return from shul to kindle the lights.

When Erev Yom Tov is on Shabbos, the candles are only lit after *tzeis hakochavim,* nightfall. One should recite בָּרוּךְ הַמַּבְדִיל בֵּין קוֹדֶשׁ לְקוֹדֶשׁ, *Blessed is He Who separates between holiness and holiness,* and then light the candles. It is forbidden to create a new flame on Yom Tov. Therefore, the candles must be lit from a preexisting flame.

When Yom Tov is on Shabbos, the candles are lit before sunset, as they are on any Erev Shabbos.

On the second of two Yom Tov nights:

❖ If the second night is a weeknight, the candles are lit only after *tzeis hakochavim,* nightfall. If the second night of Yom Tov falls out on Motza'ei Shabbos one should recite בָּרוּךְ הַמַּבְדִיל בֵּין קוֹדֶשׁ לְקוֹדֶשׁ, *Blessed is He Who separates between holiness and holiness,* and then light the candles.

When the second Yom Tov day is on Shabbos, the candles are lit before sunset, as they are on any Erev Shabbos.

It is forbidden to create a new flame on Yom Tov. Therefore, on the second night of Yom Tov the candles must be lit from a preexisting flame.

On Yom Kippur:

❖ Once the candles are lit women accept upon themselves all the restrictions of Yom Kippur and therefore must make sure to kindle the candles while wearing non-leather shoes.

For this reason, the candles are lit before sunset, in advance of the onset of Yom Kippur, as they are on Erev Shabbos. Furthermore, the candles must be lit before reciting the blessings, as on Erev Shabbos.

When to Recite the Berachah:

Rav Yosef Falk again quotes his mother Baila as opining that when Yom Tov falls out on a weekday the *berachah* should be recited first and then the candles lit. Other opinions maintain to light the candles first and then recite the *berachah,* as is done on Erev Shabbos.

The Blessings on the Yom Tov Candles

ROSH HASHANAH:

❖ On both nights of Rosh Hashanah the prevalent custom is for women to recite the *Shehecheyanu* blessing. On the second night, it is preferable that the *Shehecheyanu* blessing be recited over a new garment or a new fruit placed near the candles. If these are unavailable, the *Shehecheyanu* should still be recited at this time.

When Yom Tov coincides with Shabbos add the words in brackets.

בָּרוּךְ אַתָּה יהוה אֱלֹהֵינוּ מֶלֶךְ הָעוֹלָם, אֲשֶׁר קִדְּשָׁנוּ בְּמִצְוֹתָיו, וְצִוָּנוּ לְהַדְלִיק נֵר שֶׁל [שַׁבָּת וְשֶׁל] יוֹם טוֹב.

BORUCH ATO ADONOY ELOHAYNU MELECH HO-ŌLOM, ASHER KID'SHONU B'MITZVOSOV, V'TZIVONU L'HADLIK NAYR SHEL [SHABOS V'SHEL] YOM TOV.

*B*lessed are You, Hashem, our God, King of the universe, Who has sanctified us with His commandments, and has commanded us to kindle the light of [the Sabbath and of] Yom Tov.

בָּרוּךְ אַתָּה יהוה אֱלֹהֵינוּ מֶלֶךְ הָעוֹלָם, שֶׁהֶחֱיָנוּ וְקִיְּמָנוּ וְהִגִּיעָנוּ לַזְּמַן הַזֶּה.

BORUCH ATO ADONOY ELOHAYNU MELECH HO-ŌLOM, SHEHECHEYONU V'KIY'MANU V'HIGIONU LAZ'MAN HA-ZE.

*B*lessed are You, Hashem, our God, King of the universe, Who has kept us alive, sustained us, and brought us to this season.

YOM KIPPUR:

When Yom Tov coincides with Shabbos add the words in brackets.

בָּרוּךְ אַתָּה יהוה אֱלֹהֵינוּ מֶלֶךְ הָעוֹלָם, אֲשֶׁר קִדְּשָׁנוּ בְּמִצְוֹתָיו, וְצִוָּנוּ לְהַדְלִיק נֵר שֶׁל [שַׁבָּת וְשֶׁל] יוֹם הַכִּפּוּרִים.

BORUCH ATO ADONOY ELOHAYNU MELECH HO-ŌLOM, ASHER KID'SHONU B'MITZVOSOV, V'TZIVONU L'HADLIK NAYR SHEL [SHABOS V'SHEL] YOM HAKIPURIM.

*B*lessed are You, Hashem, our God, King of the universe, Who has sanctified us with His commandments, and has commanded us to kindle the light of [the Sabbath and of] Yom Kippur.

בָּרוּךְ אַתָּה יהוה אֱלֹהֵינוּ מֶלֶךְ הָעוֹלָם, שֶׁהֶחֱיָנוּ וְקִיְּמָנוּ וְהִגִּיעָנוּ לַזְּמַן הַזֶּה.

BORUCH ATO ADONOY ELOHAYNU MELECH HO-ŌLOM, SHEHECHEYONU V'KIY'MANU V'HIGIONU LAZ'MAN HA-ZE.

*B*lessed are You, Hashem, our God, King of the universe, Who has kept us alive, sustained us, and brought us to this season.

THE BLESSINGS ON THE YOM KIPPUR CANDLES

When Yom Kippur coincides with Shabbos
the words in brackets are added.

*B*lessed are You, Hashem, our God, King of the universe, Who has sanctified us with His commandments, and has commanded us to kindle the light of [the Sabbath and of] Yom Kippur.

*B*lessed are You, Hashem, our God, King of the universe, Who has kept us alive, sustained us, and brought us to this season.

THE BLESSINGS ON THE YOM TOV CANDLES

ROSH HASHANAH, SUCCOS, SHEMINI ATZERES/SIMCHAS TORAH, PESACH, SHAVUOS

When kindling the lights of a Festival that coincides with the Sabbath, follow the same procedure as for the Sabbath lights.

When the Festival falls on a weekday, some follow the above procedure, while others recite the blessings before lighting the candles.

When Yom Tov coincides with Shabbos, the words in brackets are added.

*B*lessed are You, Hashem, our God, King of the universe, Who has sanctified us with His commandments, and has commanded us to kindle the light of [the Sabbath and of] Yom Tov.

The following blessing is omitted on the seventh and eighth nights of Pesach

*B*lessed are You, Hashem, our God, King of the universe, Who has kept us alive, sustained us, and brought us to this season.

arranged, and with their lives on the line, dozens of concentration camp prisoners came to partake in the lighting of the first Chanukah candle.

Rabbi Yisroel Spira, the Bluzhever Rebbe (1889-1989), was chosen to recite the berachos and light the candle. With much emotion, the Rebbe recited the three berachos and lit the candle, after which everyone dispersed to get some desperately needed rest. One Jew stayed behind, approached the Rebbe, and said, "Rebbe, I believe you recited a berachah in vain." "Why?" questioned the Rebbe. "Which berachah did I recite in vain?" The man replied, "Rebbe, I understand why you recited the first berachah on the neiros, as it is a blessing upon the performance of a mitzvah, as well as the second blessing which recalls the miracle of Chanukah that took place. But how could you invoke God's Name and recite the third berachah, the berachah of Shehecheyanu, which thanks Hashem for keeping us alive and bringing us to this present time. How can we recite such a berachah when we are experiencing a living torture indescribable and unparalleled in the annals of world history?"

The Bluzhever Rebbe responded, "I, too, hesitated before reciting the third berachah of Shehecheyanu. However, when I saw the dozens of Jewish prisoners risking their lives and sacrificing their desperately needed rest, all for the privilege of partaking in the mitzvah of neiros Chanukah, I thanked Hashem. It was an appreciation for bringing me to this moment where I witnessed such an amazing and awe-inspiring moment in the history of the Jewish people. This was a moment of absolute mesirus nefesh, a moment of pure desire to fulfill the will of Hashem, a moment of pure light amid the darkness, something which I feel fortunate to have witnessed" (Ani Ma'amin, page 248; Haggadah Al Matzos U'Merorim, page 22).

PESACH, SHAVUOS, SUCCOS, SHEMINI ATZERES/SIMCHAS TORAH

On each night of Yom Tov, with the exception of the last days of Pesach, both the blessing on the candles and *Shehecheyanu* are recited.
On the last two nights of Pesach only the blessing on the candles is recited; the *Shehecheyanu* is not recited.
When Yom Tov coincides with Shabbos the words in brackets are added.

בָּרוּךְ אַתָּה יהוה אֱלֹהֵינוּ מֶלֶךְ הָעוֹלָם, אֲשֶׁר קִדְּשָׁנוּ בְּמִצְוֹתָיו, וְצִוָּנוּ לְהַדְלִיק נֵר שֶׁל [שַׁבָּת וְשֶׁל] יוֹם טוֹב.

BORUCH ATO ADONOY ELOHAYNU MELECH HO-ŌLOM, ASHER KID'SHONU B'MITZVOSOV, V'TZIVONU L'HADLIK NAYR SHEL [SHABOS V'SHEL] YOM TOV.

*B*lessed are You, Hashem, our God, King of the universe, Who has sanctified us with His commandments, and has commanded us to kindle the light of [the Sabbath and of] the Festival.

בָּרוּךְ אַתָּה יהוה אֱלֹהֵינוּ מֶלֶךְ הָעוֹלָם, שֶׁהֶחֱיָנוּ וְקִיְּמָנוּ וְהִגִּיעָנוּ לַזְּמַן הַזֶּה.

BORUCH ATO ADONOY ELOHAYNU MELECH HO-ŌLOM, SHEHECHEYONU V'KIY'MANU V'HIGIONU LAZ'MAN HA-ZE.

*B*lessed are You, Hashem, our God, King of the universe, Who has kept us alive, sustained us, and brought us to this season.

Shehecheyanu

It was the first night of Chanukah in the Bergen-Belsen concentration camp and the Jews had, with much sacrifice to their lives, procured a small candle that would be used for the mitzvah of neiros Chanukah. A predetermined time was